ISLAMIC
CULTURE

A STUDY OF CULTURAL ANTHROPOLOGY

FARID YOUNOS

author HOUSE®

AuthorHouse™
1663 Liberty Drive
Bloomington, IN 47403
www.authorhouse.com
Phone: 1-800-839-8640

cover photo credit: "Nastaran Qassemi praying at the age of 3."

Published by AuthorHouse 11/08/2013

ISBN: 978-1-4918-2344-6 (sc)
ISBN: 978-1-4918-2343-9 (e)

Library of Congress Control Number: 2013917735

In the name of the only One who created
mankind and diversity.

Dedicated to Professor Hanif Sherali and
Mrs. Semeen Sherali

Without your support, feedback, and
encouragement during the last 34 years, I wouldn't
be where I am today. Thank you.

Table of Contents

Acknowledgement

It was a great honor and privilege to be selected to teach Cultural Anthropology of the Middle East at California State University, East Bay in 2005. Based upon Professor of Anthropology Laurie Price's suggestion, Professor Beeson, the Chairman of the Department of Sociology and Anthropology, called and offered me the job. I was thrilled. Not only because I was selected, but also because I could do something in the area of Islamic Anthropology while teaching. When I started teaching, I noticed that not much had been done in the field of Cultural Anthropology of Islam. Of course, Islamic Culture has been illustrated before, and there are many books, however not under the title 'Islamic Culture'. There are several books discussing anthropological aspects of Islamic life, but not specifically under Islamic Culture; such as *Toward Islamic Anthropology* by Professor Akbar S. Ahmed (1986) based on western anthropological study, with an emphasis on theory. *The Anthropology of Islam* by Gabriele Marranci (2008) discusses contemporary Islam and relates to current affairs. Teaching at Cal State, East Bay, and noticing the lack of such an important field, made me decide to write about the Cultural Anthropology of Islam. I am very grateful to Professor Price and Professor Beeson who gave me the opportunity to teach in this field. I am indebted to my students that they raised and debated many questions concerning Islamic Culture in class. They made me think more seriously about these issues and enlightened me with their feedback. In the last five years, I have discussed many of these issues on my talk show on television at Nooor TV. My world wide audience not only give me their feedback and support, but also offer their criticism, forcing me to rethink and research more on the issue of Islamic Culture. The whole project was organized and polished by my Research Assistant Morwarid Hatef, a graduate of the University of California, Davis. She has been a great help in providing feedback and new concepts to be included in this project. I am not only grateful and thankful to Morwarid for her assistance, but honestly admit that without her support I would not have been able to complete this project. And, as always, my wife Fowzia Younos who has been a great support, both socially and financially. I owe all of my achievements, academically and personally, to her and I thank her from the bottom of my heart for being a great support.

Introduction

Anthropology, the study of man, began in the 19th century, particularly during the colonial period. Anthropos is a Greek word meaning man. It is a field of study that deals with all aspects of human existence. In this study, we study the Cultural Anthropology of Islam. The difference between social anthropology and cultural anthropology is that in social anthropology, anthropologists deal with social institutions and their interrelated principles, while cultural anthropology deals not necessarily with the structural form of societies but how people base their daily lives and emerge as a group with certain value systems. It must be noted that cultural anthropology is based upon non-empirical principles, where things can simply be observed. Both social anthropologists and cultural anthropologists are interested in how people live. But as stated, the social interaction of people as political interaction is different than what people believe and how they conduct individual interactions with the social system. Our task in this study is different than the main anthropological studies that deal with metaphysical principles of anthropology- that is the belief system of a group of people that comprise 1.7 billion adherents worldwide. To proceed in this field of study, namely Cultural Anthropology of Islam, we must define what culture is from an Islamic perspective. Also, an attempt has been made to stay away from Islamic sociology and history. To study Islamic sociology please refer to my previous book, "The Principle of Islamic Sociology". The following are four fields of anthropological studies: biological anthropology, cultural anthropology, archeological anthropology, and linguistic anthropology. Our study focuses on cultural anthropology that is the study of Muslims, including their norms and values based upon the tradition of the Prophet. Also, because the language of the Qur'an is in Arabic, and Arabic is the core principle of Islamic linguistic anthropology, we will briefly touch on the language of the Qur'an. Anthropologists define language as a set of symbols that convey meaning. Interestingly enough, Ayah (verse) means symbol. That tells us that the Qur'an, from a linguistic point of view, is a symbolic book and God conveys His message by symbols.

PART ONE

ANTHROPOLOGICAL ASPECTS OF ISLAMIC CULTURE

ISLAMIC CULTURAL ANTHROPOLOGY

Today, the world of Islam is one of the most sophisticated communities in the world, with 1.7 billion adherents; that is one-fifth of the world's population. Muslims live in forty-four countries, from the Atlantic coast of Africa, Middle East, Central Asia, such as Afghanistan and the Indian subcontinent, to Asia. Muslims are found all over the world due to migration, labor, and obtaining an education. There are six million Muslims living in Europe and six to seven million living in the United States. Muslims in non-Muslim countries not only integrated, but also became an issue of coexistence among non-Muslims for policy makers and governments. Although Muslims have been in non-Muslim countries for more than a hundred years now, they still are not accepted by mainstream culture. This is due to a lack of knowledge about Islam, media biases about Islam and also because Muslims do not want to change without violating the principles of the Qur'an and the tradition of the Prophet. While I am writing this book, Islamaphobia is on the rise in European countries as well as in the United States and Canada, as well as Danish cartoons portraying the Prophet Mohammed. It is important to note that the Islamaphobic attitude has not been an issue due to the September 11, 2001 tragedy; it existed before in a variety of degrees. However, 9/11 made it much stronger against Muslims. In order to have a peaceful coexistence, non-Muslims should learn more about the Islamic culture and Muslims should also change their lifestyle for the sake of progress and the sake of Islam. Islamic law has the potential to accommodate itself based upon the needs and necessities of the time we live in. Another issue with Islamophobia is the stand that non-Muslim governments take against Muslims, directly or indirectly, abandoning Islamic movements. An example is the Islamic political movement of Algeria, where a democratic Islamic government was toppled by outside forces. The democratic election of Hamas in Palestine was also not acknowledged by the West. Official Islamophobia by non-Muslim governments causes radicalism and terrorism.

CULTURE DEFINED

So far, anthropologists have come up with 164 definitions of culture. In Islam, since a human being is part of a universal system and a universal system is part of a human being, the definition of culture is a natural phenomenon. Human culture, just like enzyme culture, is a phenomenon of growth. This means that the culture of Islam is not a concept of static principle but rather moving, growing, and developing. This means that, for Muslims, culture is not just a tradition or a ritual that never changes, rather, they can change culturally with the time and space they live in. In the study of human development, we see that biologically a human grows, however, at the same time, humans also have the capacity to grow culturally and change culturally to fit needs or desires. Islamic anthropology shares three views of culture: idealism, behaviorism, and holism. To be clear, idealism means shared ways of thinking. In Islam, the Islamic idealism is Tawhid, or Oneness of God, man and universe. Behaviorism is sharing ways of behaving. Islamic behaviorism is to follow the traditions of Prophet Mohammed. And finally, holism, which are ways of thinking and behaving. Islamic holism is to follow the guidance of the Qur'an as a core principle of thinking and follow the footsteps of the Messenger as a role model for behavior which give us Islamic Culture. Cultural anthropologists studied Muslim societies from an ethnographical point of view without questioning the roots and reasons of the cultural act. In this study, we have tried not only to show the cultural principles of Islam, but also, to the best of our ability, elaborate on the reason for a cultural act. This elaboration on reasons for the cultural act makes the study of Islamic Cultural Anthropology very interesting.

TAWHID: ORIGIN OF ISLAMIC ANTHROPOLOGY

To fully understand Islam, and become convinced that Islam is a way of life, one has to know the principle of Tawhid, which is the foundation Islamic life is based upon. Tawhid means oneness. It entails that God is one, the universe is one, mankind is one, and knowledge is one. God, in Islam, is a being that does not have a similar or associate; He is the one who created the whole universal system. He has the power to sustain, protect, and recreate His own creations. He is absolute and He is absolute just. In Tawhid there is no duality or discrimination. The whole universal system has been created on a balance and they are interrelated to one another. The main core principle of Tawhid is oneness of God Himself and He states: "Say: He is God. One. God, the Everlasting Refuge. He does not beget. Nor is He begotten. And comparable to Him, there is none."(Qur'an 112:1, 2, 3, 4)[1] According to Tawhid, the Qur'an witnesses a scientific fact that the entire universal system is in balance, and all components of creation align with one another for harmony and peace. The Qur'an states: "And as to the sky- it is He alone who has raised it. Thus it is He alone who has set the balance of all things, so that you might not transgress the just balance.

---

[1] Qur'an 112:1,2,3,4

Therefore, shall you establish weights and measures with justice. And you shall not by fraud diminish the balance. And as to the Earth- it is He alone who has laid it down for all living creatures." (Qur'an 55:7,8,9,10)[2]

Deoxyribonucleic Acid, known as DNA, are the building blocks and shape of DNA molecules in humans, plants and every living thing. The genetic makeup of DNA can be found in both plants and humans, which begins in the formation of a "Double helix". DNA in vegetation, as well as human beings, shares the same genetic base pairs (A,C,G,T), which accounts for proteins that exist in our bodies and governs functions for human living properties. Also, DNA is built of nucleotides, which are adenine, cytosine, guanine, and thymine. These genetic codes that are stored within DNA, express a sequence that dictates what will take form in plants, animals or human beings. As a matter of fact, DNA is a common thread that connects all living organisms. We conclude that according to Tawhid, Law of Nature and Law of Allah are one and the same. Since mankind is part of the natural system and the natural system is part of human beings, human beings accordingly are a natural entity and He must be one, too. The Qur'an states: "O humankind! Be ever God-fearing, conscious of your Lord who created all of you from a single soul." (Qur'an 4:1)[3] The term "single soul" in Arabic, according to the text of the Qur'an, is *Nafis e Wahid*, and that is the oneness of man in the universal system. So God is one and He created human beings as one natural entity. If we look at the definition of Islam, which means submission to the will of Allah, Islam also means peace, which has been derived from the root word of *Salama*. What this definition tells us is that no one can have peace and harmony unless the whole system of living

---

[2] Qur'an 55:7,8,9,10
[3] Qur'an 4:1

beings are aligned with the natural law, Tawhid. From a psychological point of view, one can only have peace in his heart if he fully submits to Allah, which scientifically is the law of nature. Thus, we see that the two definitions join as one principle of oneness, and that is submission. It is understandable that the One who has created the system must give its creation laws to be governed by. Therefore, Allah has given laws to the entire universal system for the sustaining and smooth functioning of His creation, and since mankind is part of this creation, He also blessed him with the Qur'an as human laws. Allah is the law giver for His entire creation. According to Islam, in the principle of Tawhid, if we align our work based upon the Qur'an, then everything will run naturally; however, if we stay away from the Qur'an (the main source of law), then we go astray. We not only cause damage to ourselves, but also to His creation, such as polluting the water and air. The Qur'an states: "That God alone is powerful over all things, and that God alone has truly encompassed all things in knowledge." (Qur'an 65:12)[4]

ABRAHAM, THE PROGENITOR: A STUDY OF GENEALOGY

The pilgrimage to Mecca is to commemorate the remembrance of Prophet Abraham (Ibrahim in Arabic), who is the progenitor of the three monotheistic faiths: Judaism, Christianity, and Islam.

The Jewish faith recognizes Prophet Abraham as the progenitor of the Hebrew people, while the Christians see him as a

---

[4] Qur'an 65:12

patriarch, a biblical Prophet, or just a biblical figure. Yet, they fail to recognize him as the founder of monotheism.

According to Islam, the Hebrew people are descendants of Isaac, and the Arabs are the descendants of Ismail. Both sons of Prophet Abraham were Prophets. Therefore, Prophet Abraham is the progenitor of the Prophets. Second, it was through these two Prophets that different Arab and Jewish tribes developed. Therefore, Prophet Abraham is the progenitor of all the different tribes. Allah states in the Qur'an: "Say ye: We believe in Allah and the revelation given to us, and to Abraham, Ismail, Isaac, Jacob and the tribes, and that given to Moses and Jesus, and that given to (all) Prophets from their Lord: We make no difference between one and another of them: And we bow to Allah (in Islam)." (Qur'an 2:135)[5]

It is equally important to note that our Jewish and Christian counterparts fail to recognize that Islam is a continuation of previous faiths, not a separate religion. In fact, their books foretold the coming of Prophet Mohammad, but rejected him; even though they saw the sign of his Prophethood. In the Bible, it states: "I will raise up for them a Prophet like you from among their brothers; I will put my words in his mouth, and he will tell them everything I command him." (Deuteronomy 18:18); and "Or if you give the scroll to someone who cannot read, and say, "Read this, please," he will answer, "I don't know how to read." (Isaiah 29:18) Allah states in the Qur'an: "They say: Become Jews or Christians if ye would be guided (to salvation). Say thou Nay! (I would rather) the religion of Abraham, the true, and he joined not gods with Allah." (Qur'an 2:135) Third, Prophet Abraham is the spiritual progenitor of the believing people. He is the father of monotheistic religions, a trust that was passed

---

[5] Qur'an 2:135

onto Muslims after Prophet Mohammad. The Qur'an alludes to this saying: "That the Messenger may be a witness for you, and ye be witnesses for mankind." The Qur'an also states in the same verse: "He has chosen you, and has imposed no difficulties on you in religion; it is the cult of your father Abraham." (Qur'an 22:78)[6] Prophet Abraham was neither a Jew nor a Christian, but a Muslim who had submitted to the Will of Allah. He taught humanity that God is one, mankind is one, knowledge is one, and the universe is one. The Qur'an states: "Abraham was not a Jew nor a Christian; but he was true in faith and bowed his will to Allah's (which is Islam) and he joined not gods with Allah." The next verse continues: "Without doubt among men, the nearest of kin to Abraham are those who follow him." (Qur'an 3:67 & 68)[7]

Allah loved Prophet Abraham and chose him as His friend. Allah states in the Qur'an: "Who can be better in religion than one who submits his whole self to Allah, does good, and follows the way of Abraham the true faith: For Allah did take Abraham for a friend." (Qur'an 4:125)[8]

It is because of this highest position of Prophet Abraham that Muslims send peace and blessings to Prophet Abraham several times a day in their daily prayers, alongside Prophet Mohammad. This association between Prophet Abraham and the seal of Prophets, Prophet Mohammad, not only establishes finalization of Prophethood, but completes a historical link of monotheistic religions through a chain of Prophets.

WHAT IS THAT ?

The legacy of Prophet Abraham to humanity is very simple: That God is one and submission is due to Him alone, and His

---

[6] Qur'an 22:78
[7] Qur'an 3:67 & 68
[8] Qur'an 4:125

obedience must have the highest priority for mankind in all aspects of life.

For certain, Prophet Abraham was a model of submission and obedience to his Creator. Allah states in the Qur'an: "Abraham was indeed a model, devoutly obedient to Allah (and) true in faith, and he joined not gods with Allah." (Qur'an 6:22)[9]

According to historical data, Prophet Abraham preached monotheism a thousand years before Judaism, Christianity, and Islam. And after all these years, Muslims are the only monotheistic faith on the face of this Earth that commemorate Prophet Abraham's legacy and obey God's order to do the pilgrimage as Abraham did and follow his way. Prophet Abraham is not only the progenitor of the three monotheistic religions, but the founder of Islam.

THE QUR'AN: A STUDY OF LINGUISTIC ANTHROPOLOGY

The Qur'an, which means Reading or Recital, was revealed to Prophet Mohammed in 610 A.D in Arabic. This was because of the richness of the Arabic language in terms of grammar 'structure' and precision. Allah states: "We have made it a Qur'an in Arabic that Ye may be able to understand (and learn wisdom)." (Qur'an 43:3)[10] Our Creator also says that: "Verily we have made this Qur'an easy in thy tongue in order that they may give heed." (Qur'an 44:58)[11] After the advent of

---

[9] Qur'an 6:22
[10] Qur'an 43:3
[11] Qur'an 44:58

Qur'an in Arabic?
I thought it was
in symbols –

Islam, the Arabic language became the dominant social force within Arab society, and later among non-Arab nations who adopted Islam as their religion.

To Muslims, the Qur'an is the word of God, the Divine Language, the language of power and beauty. For Muslim and non-Muslim linguists, it is the most highly literal and poetic (although the Qur'an is not poetry) language ever known in human history. Reading it comforts the soul and mind. The language of the Qur'an not only changed the culture and outlook of a nation of mainly Bedouins, but made them achieve one of the most astonishing civilizations in human history.

The Qur'an itself challenged Arab non-believers who accused the last messenger of God, Prophet Mohammed, of reporting words invented by human beings just to imitate a chapter of the Qur'an as though he forged it: "Bring then a Surah (Chapter) like unto it and call to your aid anyone you can." (Qur'an 10:38)[12] No Arab or non-Arab poet, writer, or eloquent preacher has been able to imitate the Qur'an. This "inimitability" is one of the characteristics or the miraculous signs (I'jaz) of Qur'anic language.

The translation of the Qur'an in other languages of humanity is allowed only for enabling non-Arabs to understand the meaning of the Divine language text. The first translation was in Farsi (Persian) in the fourth century of Hijra, but even Arabs needed to read the tafseer (interpretation and commentary) of the Qur'an; where the tafseer is the word of human beings. In studying the language of the Qur'an the most interesting phenomenon one faces is the authenticity of the Qur'an. For more than 1400 years it has remained untouched. The main reason for this is that Allah intended to preserve His revelation.

---

[12] Qur'an 10:38

The Qur'an states: "We have without doubt, sent down the message and we will assuredly guard it from corruption." (Qur'an 15:9)[13] Allah speaks about the glory and authenticity of the Qur'an by stating: "Nay, this is a glorious reading on a preserved tablet." Also, He reminds people about the Qur'an saying, "This is a glorious reading in a book well-kept which none but the purified touch. This is a revelation of the Lord of the World." (Qur'an 56:77-80)[14] The language of the Qur'an, is highly literal, as it concerns as much with facts of life, and also deals with day to day functions of life- individually and collectively. It tells you about human weaknesses and strengths. It also comforts the soul and heals the heart. It has never been, and never will be, an old book because it interprets itself according to current time.

The Qur'an is also a symbolic language. It represents itself to humanity as a book of signs. As a matter of fact, "ayah", which has been translated as verse, also means sign. Allah states: "We have indeed made clear the signs unto any people who hold firmly to faith." (Qur'an 2:118)[15] The Creator of the universe alludes to mankind by stating: "behold thy creation of the heavens and the Earth and the alteration of night and day there are indeed signs for man of understanding." (Qur'an 3:190)[16] Cleary, in *The Essential Koran*, states:

"Arabic, most precise and primitive of the Semitic languages, shows signs of being originally a constructed language. It is built upon mathematical principles- A phenomenon not paralleled by any other language...For the Sufis of the classical period, the Koran is the encoded document which

---

[13] Qur'an 15:9
[14] Qur'an 56:77-80
[15] Qur'an 2:118
[16] Qur'an 3:190

contains Sufi teachings. Theologians tend to assume that it is capable of interpretation only in a conventionally religious way; historians are inclined to look for earlier literary or religious sources; others for evidence of contemporary events reflected in its pages. For the Sufi, the Koran is a document with numerous levels of transmission, each one of which has a meaning in accordance with the capacity for understanding of the reader. It is this attitude toward the book which made possible the understanding between people who were of nominally Christian, pagan, or Jewish backgrounds- a feeling which the orthodox could not understand. The Koran in one sense is therefore a document of psychological importance."[17]

MOHAMMED: THE FOUNDER OF ISLAMIC CULTURE

In most societies, culture is inherited from generation to generation. However, in Islam, the founder of Islamic culture, Mohammed, formulated Islamic culture for his followers. He did not inherit the Islamic culture from his ancestors, rather he formulated his culture based upon the revelation he received from God. His tradition, which is called the Sunnah, established a complete way of life that encompasses not only daily rituals, because Islam is not rituals alone, but also principles of life that make humanity grow to the highest level possible. A Muslim has the potential to either reach the highest lord by following the culture of Mohammed or becoming the lowest of the low due to ignorance of the Qur'an and the traditions of the Prophet. Islamic culture does not deal with daily routines, but surprisingly

---

[17] Cleary, Thomas. *The Essential Koran*. San Francisco: Harper, 1993.

formulates a person's inner and outer actions and behavior. Hence, Islamic culture is a socio-psychological principle that deals with behavior as well as inner soul satisfaction and felicity. Islamic culture stands on the basis of intelligence, belief and action. It is the intelligence of a person who wants to absorb the teachings of Mohammed. It is through his or her intelligence that he formulates his belief system. The combination of intelligence and belief gives him or her an Islamic civilized culture. This culture is designed to make him grow, succeed, and prosper. Thus, if one does not use his intelligence properly, and does not incorporate his intelligence with his belief system, he will not practice an Islamic culture. The formula is:

Intelligence + Belief + Action= Civilized Islamic Culture

Cultural Anthropology of Islam

Having said the above, Islamic Cultural Anthropology has been designed by Almighty God and put into practice through His noble Prophet. In order to understand Islamic culture, one has to resort to the Qur'an and the traditions of the Prophet. It is important to note that the Qur'an is guidance for humanity, and the traditions of the Prophet, in this case, is the culture giver. The Qur'an clearly indicates different tasks for Islamic life, such as prayer, charity due, performing Hajj, and so forth. The Prophet's traditions, manners, and words reveal how to do things culturally. Therefore, Cultural Anthropology in Islam is not similar to studying a tribe or an ethnic group, rather, a complete way of life as one single package that all came from the Qur'an and Mohammed based upon the principle of Tawhid. Anything outside the Qur'an and the traditions of the Prophet, is not Islamic culture, but the traditions and indigenous customs of certain societies and communities. "For the Muslim, rules of marriage, inheritance, and an entire code covering the most intimate details of human behavior- are laid down explicitly. The organization of society and the behavior of its members are predetermined. For Muslims, therefore, the dilemmas of this world are reduced. Man's mission is to reconcile society with the instructions of God." (Akbar S. Ahmed: 57[18])

Mohammed was born in 570 A.D. He lost his parents at a very early age and was raised by his grandfather, the Chief of the Quraish family. Mohammed was unlettered, meaning he was not able to read or write, but he possessed a high culture. At the age of 25, he married a business woman and widow named Khadija, who was more than 15 years older than him. After pondering many years in the cave of Hera in western Arabia, he received revelation from God through Angel Gabriel. This revelation changed the world politically, economically, socially and psychologically.

The First Revelation

The first revelation has significant biological, educational and philosophical principles. It stated: "Read! In the name of your Lord who created: He created man from a clot. Read! Your Lord Is the Most Bountiful One who taught by pen, who taught man what he did not know." (Qur'an 96:1-5)[19] First, the revelation said "Read". This principle, to read, made knowledge the foundation of Islam. Second, the verse reveals that humanity is created from a blood clot. This principle rejects social Darwinism and from the very beginning alludes to creation of humanity by God. Third, the same verse tells us that human beings can achieve their goals through the generosity of their Creator by relying on the pen.

Mohammed could not read/write but, he introduced the Qur'an? he interpreted the Qur'an.

[18] Akbar S. Ahmed:57
[19] Qur'an 96:1-5

Culturally, Prophet Mohammed either received revelation or was inspired by God. Thus, nothing actually came from his own mind. Later, the Qur'an stated: "We have indeed, in the Messenger of Allah, a beautiful pattern (of conduct)." (Qur'an 33:21)[20]

From a cultural anthropological point of view, the above verse makes Mohammed not only a spiritual figure; but also a leader and example for all aspects of life. His words (Hadith) and his actions (Sunnah) are the role models for the Muslim culture for the last 1400 years. Additionally, his family life and the lives of his beloved wives and daughter, Fatima, and his son-in-law and cousin Ali, and his grandchildren, Hassan and Hussein, became role models of conduct, behavior, manners and leadership for the Muslim Ummah (Community). His role as the first interpreter of the Qur'an and an application of the Qur'an in daily lives of Muslims, founded the Islamic values, norms, and principles. In Islam, laws are derived not only from the Qur'an, but also from the traditions and sayings of the Prophet. Mohammed emerged as a Prophet of God engulfed with leadership, statesman, father, grandfather, community member, negotiator, and as a complete guide for humanity.

Within less than a hundred years, Islam spread westward and eastward as Napoleon Bonaparte said, "Mohammed was a prince; he gathered his compatriots around himself and in a few years they conquered half the world. In fifteen years they tore more souls from false gods, knocked over more idols, and destroyed more pagan temples than did the followers of Moses and Jesus Christ in fifteen centuries. Mohammed was a great man" (Napoleon Bonaparte (1769-1821).

---

[20] Qur'an 33:21

Emigration to Medina

Emigration in Islamic culture is the most important aspect of the Islamic civilization. Emigration to Muslims is to awaken and learn challenges and prepare for a civilized life. It is only through emigration that man achieves his highest level of his potential. Civilization came into existence because of emigration. Mohammed came under extreme pressure by opposition forces, his own tribe, to the extent that they wanted to kill him. Mohammed was commanded by God to leave Mecca and go to Yathrib, present day Medina. The Arab tribes of Yathrib welcomed Mohammed and saw him as a good community arbiter of peace among different ethnic groups in the area.

WHY? 2°

CENTERS OF CULTURAL DEVELOPMENT: MECCA, MEDINA, AND JERUSALEM

Mecca

Mecca is the first important city in Islamic culture. It was in this city that the Prophet of Islam was born and it was in the same city that the first revelation of the Qur'an to mankind appeared. Muslims believe that anyone who performs Hajj that is accepted is like a new born baby because a trip to Ka'aba can potentially rinse away all sins. It is located in the west of Saudi Arabia in the valley of Hijaz. It is the only city required by all able Muslims to be visited at least once in their lifetime and circumambulate the House of God. This city has been mentioned in the Qur'an as follows: "For He is the One who pacified the disbelievers and held back their hands from harming you-and your hands from them- in proximity to the valley of Mecca at

Hudaybiyyah, after you captured their advance forces and He made you triumph over them. And ever is God all-seeing of all that you do." (Qur'an 48:24)[21] It has also been mentioned as Bakkah in the Qur'an, "Indeed, the first House of God appointed for all people is that in the valley of Bakkah. It is most blessed and a source of guidance for all the peoples of the world." (Qur'an 3:96)[22] The word Bakkah means to crash or annihilate. It is named as such because it annihilates tyranny, arrogance, selfishness, and egoism. The city is also called Um Al Qura, mother of all cities. The latitude of Mecca is 21 degrees 25' 19" N and longitude is 39 degrees 49' 46" E. Muslim scholars believe that the Ka'aba is the focal point of the Earth. For performing ritual prayers, 1.7 billion Muslims face the direction of Ka'aba. Um in Arabic also means facing a particular direction. It is also called Al Baladul Amin, the faithful city. It is in this city that the Ka'aba was built. It has been reported that the Ka'aba was built by Adam and rebuilt by Abraham and his son Ismail; it has been renovated several times during the course of history. According to Islamic history, the Black Stone on the southern part of the Ka'aba, about 1.1 meters above the ground, is believed to come from heaven or from the "heavens" as a meteorite, which indicated to Prophet Abraham where to construct the Ka'aba. There are not one, but eight pieces. It has been reported that the Prophet of Islam stated that the black stone came from heaven and was whiter than milk, but the sins of mankind made it dark. Muslims start their tawaf (circulation) and circumbulation from this point of the stone and end it at the same point. Another important feature of the Ka'aba is the position of Abraham, which has been mentioned in the Qur'an. This is called Maqam because Abraham stood there on a piece of stone to build the walls of Ka'aba. The virtue of it, is that

---

[21] Qur'an 48:24
[22] Qur'an 3:96

Abraham, the father of monotheism, prayed to God almighty. The Qur'an states: "So behold! We made the Sacred House in Mecca a spiritual resort and place of security for all believing people. So take up the marked Station of Abraham there, as a place of Prayer. Moreover, We covenanted with Abraham and Ishmael: You shall purify My House for all those who shall circumambulate it in worship; and for all those who shall retreat there; and for all those who shall both bow, and bow their faces down to the ground, in Prayer there. And behold! Abraham said in supplication: My lord! Make this land of Mecca secure. And provide its people with every kind of fruit- such of them as believe in God and in the coming Judgment of the Last Day." (Qur'an 2:125,126)[23]

Medina

Medina is the second most important city in Islamic culture, and has also been reported, according to Prophet Mohammed, to be a sacred territory. The Prophet of Islam reportedly offered supplication for Medina, stating: "Oh Allah! Make Medina as beloved to us as you made Mecca beloved or more than that, make it conducive to health and grant blessings and in its Sa' and in its mud."(Sahih Bakhuri Hadith 1889)[24] This city was called Yathrib before the migration of the Prophet. The Prophet of Islam called this place Tayeba, which means cleansing. It has also been reported that Dajjal (Antichrist) shall not enter Medina. Most civic laws of Islam were revealed in this city. One of the outstanding monuments of this city is the Prophet's Mosque. Also, when the Prophet of Islam migrated to Medina, he built the mosque of Quba and that is the first mosque

---

[23] Qur'an 2:125,126
[24] Sahih Al Bukhari Hadith 1889

built by the Prophet of Islam. Mohammed changed the name of Yathrib to Medina. Medina means "The City". This conversion of Yathrib to Medina conveyed a message to Muslims that they were now living a city life, leaving tribal attitudes, arrogant mentalities, biases, and discrimination behind. It was in Medina that metropolitan and cosmopolitan urban life began for Muslims. In Medina, there was no discrimination and Mohammed declared men and women equal. The first political and social brotherhood and sisterhood of Islam also took shape and was established in Medina. No man had superiority over a woman and no woman had any superiority over a man. No tribe or race had superiority over another and everyone was considered and declared equal in the site of law and God. Surah Nisa (women), which was revealed in Medina, declared the equality of men and women as follows:

"O mankind! Revere your Guardian-Lord who created you from a single person. Created, of like nature, his mate, and from them twain, scattered (like seeds) countless men and women- fear Allah, through Whom ye demand your mutual (rights), and (reverence) the wombs, (that bore you): for Allah, ever watches over you." (Qur'an 4:1)[25]

By the same token, the Qur'an declared all people equal and recognized them not by race, gender, social status, or wealth, but by piety and righteousness.

"O mankind! We created you from a single (pair) of a male and a female and made you into nations and tribes, that ye may know each other (not that ye may despise) (each other). Verily the most honored of you in the sight of Allah is (he who

---

[25] Qur'an 4:1

is) the most righteous of you. And Allah has full knowledge and is well-acquainted (with all things)." (Qur'an 49:13)[26]

The importance of the above verse from a cultural and anthropological point of view is that no society will develop and reach its maximum potential if there is gender discrimination in that society. Therefore, in order to have a civil society, the prerequisite is to have equality between men and women; this was achieved for the first time in the history of mankind in Medina by the Prophet. The second principle, after gender equality, is the rule of law that Mohammed achieved when he established Medina as a civic society and justice was the prime issue for all citizens, Muslims and non-Muslims. As Professor Boisard writes in his book *Humanism in Islam:* "The law determines the basic relations of man to God, with regard to his fellowmen, and to himself. It has left nothing to chance, in a specific manner defining what is compulsory, recommended, legal, tolerated, or strictly prohibited. It embraces the body of duties imposed upon the Muslim. In his threefold capacity as believer, man, and citizen. Surrender to the law and the desire to respect its conditions are derived from the acceptance of the faith which imposes a general conception of society and of its development."(p.34)[27]

Jerusalem

After Mecca and Medina, Jerusalem is considered the third holiest city to Muslims. Jerusalem is also considered to be the first Qibla, the direction Muslims face during prayer. It was many years into the Islamic mission (16 months after the Hijrah), that Mohammed was instructed to change the Qibla from

---

[26]Qur'an 49:13
[27] Boisard, *Humanism In Islam*

Jerusalem to Mecca (Qur'an 2:142-144)[28]. It is reported that the Prophet Mohammed said, "There are only three mosques to which you should embark on a journey: the sacred mosque (Mecca, Saudi Arabia), this mosque of mine (Medina, Saudi Arabia), and the mosque of Al-Aqsa (Jerusalem)." Jerusalem is also significant because it is the place of Prophet Mohammed's miraculous night journey from Jerusalem to his ascension to Heaven. This event is mentioned in the Qur'an in the first verse of Chapter 17: "Glory be to Him, who carried His servant by night from the Holy Mosque to the Further Mosque *(al-Masjid al-Aqsa),* the precincts of which We have blessed, that We might show him some of our signs." In the night journey *(al-Isra'wal Mi'raj),* Mohammed was transported on a winged horse from Mecca to Jerusalem where he led several Prophets in prayer. Afterwards, Mohammed ascended to heaven, accompanied by the archangel Gabriel. In this journey of ascension, Mohammed passed through the seven heavens where he encountered earlier Prophets, including Jesus, Moses, and Abraham. The Dome of the Rock is the site from which Mohammed ascended.[29]

---

[28] Qur'an 2:142-144
[29] http://www.pij.org/details.php?id=646

PART TWO

MULTICULTURALISM
— IN ISLAM

In order to understand multiculturalism in Islam, one has to understand creation. According to Islam, Allah created the entire universe, and mankind is included in this creation. God says in the Qur'an, "He is the One who created for you all that is in the Earth. Then He directed Himself toward the heaven, and He fashioned it into seven heavens. For He alone is all-knowing of all things."(Qur'an 2:29)[30] Since man and the universe have been created by God, according to Islam, then the law of nature and the law of God is one and the same. Human beings are part of this natural system and the natural system is part of human beings. Therefore, human beings are a natural entity and since human beings are created from Earth, as the Qur'an states: "He alone has created man from a clay like that of fashioned pottery."(Qur'an 55:14)[31] According to Tawhid, God is One and the universe is one. The relationship of God to His creation is Oneness. This means that the entire system of creating human beings has only one origin and that is Allah, who is One. He also created human beings from a single soul saying, "O humankind! Be ever God-fearing, conscious of your Lord who created all of you from a single soul."(Qur'an 4:1)[32] This verse clearly shows the universality of human beings in the entire creation that God Almighty, who is One, created His *Khalifa* also from a single soul. This simply means there is no duality and discrimination in the creation of human beings. Nature, as we see it, is very diverse, with different colors, landscapes, climates, and topography. As such, human beings are an integrated part of the system and must be diverse in color, language, race, and thoughts. Human beings, as a diverse cultural entity, must also correspond, match, and be aligned with creation. The Qur'an states: "And of His wondrous signs is the creation of the heavens

---

[30] Qur'an 2:29
[31] Qur'an 55:14
[32] Qur'an 4:1

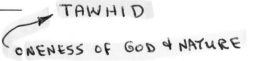
TAWHID
ONENESS OF GOD & NATURE

and the Earth and the variety of your tongues and your colors. Indeed, in all of this there are sure signs for a people of knowledge." (Qur'an 30:22)[33] Also: "O humankind! Indeed, We have created all of you from a single male and female. Moreover, We have made you peoples and tribes, so that you may know one another. And indeed, the noblest of you, in the sight of God, is the most God-fearing of you. Indeed, God is all-knowing, all-aware." (Qur'an 49:13)[34]

THE EMERGENCE OF SUNNI AND SHIA SECTS

The two sects of Islamic faith, Sunni and Shia, both emerged after the passing of the Prophet of Islam. The sects of Sunni and Shia were not a big issue during the time of the four righteous Caliphs. However, at the time of the Prophet's demise after his burial, a disagreement emerged among Muslims as to who should be head of state. Upon the death of the Prophet, people gathered at a meeting called Saqifa and after a long debate between the Companions, who were called friends and immigrants, Abu Bakr rose up and stated that the Caliph (position) must be in the hands of the Quraish tribe. At this time, Ali, the Prophet's cousin and son-in-law, with a few other companions, were at the residence of the Prophet preparing for the funeral. This means that Ali was not present at the Saqifa meeting and Ali did not pledge allegiance to Abu Bakr because he was not present at the meeting. Also, Ali's wife, Fatima, the daughter of the Prophet, asked for her inheritance but the Caliph, Abu Bakr, denied that right of inheritance to Fatima on the basis

---

[33] Qur'an 30:22
[34] Qur'an 49:13

PROPHET OF ISLAM

of the saying of the Prophet that no one inherits from Prophets. This was the first cause of the split between Muslims as Shia and Sunni. Another cause of the split between Shia and Sunni was the vengeance of Uthman, who was the third Caliph. There was a group of Muslims asking Ali, the fourth Caliph after Uthman, to capture and punish the assassins of Uthman. Ali refused to take action and thus, caused not only trouble but rebellion against him. Most prominent companions of the Prophet, such as Talha and Zobayr, joined Aisha, the Prophet's wife, against Ali. The last reason for the split was the martyrdom of Imam Hussain at Karbala. Shia means follower; in this case, the follower of Ali. Sunni comes from Sunnah, which means tradition and applies to those who follow the tradition of the Prophet. It is important to note, as we stated earlier, that Ali did pledge allegiance to Abu Bakr after the death of his wife Fatima. The reason the head of state was selected so quickly was because there were many animosities among the different tribes in the region, and each tribe wanted to be head of state. Therefore, according to most scholars, it had been appropriate to contain fires of animosity over khilafat and Abu Bakr becoming the first heads of state because they were highly respected. The Prophet married his daughter. He was the closest companion of the Prophet and joined the Prophet on his migration from Mecca to Medina. The Prophet asked him to lead prayers in his masjid during his final days when he was too ill to do so himself. Omar, who was a powerful political figure, was the first person who extended his allegiance to Abu Bakr. Ali did cooperate with all heads of state until he got elected as the head of state. During his reign, and before that, the issue of Sunni and Shia was not an issue until the martyrdom of Imam Hussain, the son of Ali, at Karbala. After this martyrdom, the issue and emergence of Shia, as a religious and political force, became very prominent.

CALIPH

KHILAFAT

Sunni Islam

Sunni Muslims comprise 80% of the Muslim population and are called Ahle Al Sunnah wa Al Jamaa, the people of tradition and congregation. They follow the Qur'an and the traditions of the Prophet. After the Qur'an, their second source of law is the Hadith and Sunnah (sayings and traditions of the Prophet). However, they believe in interpretation and application of the Qur'an and Sunnah.

THE EMERGENCE OF THE ULEMA (MEN OF KNOWLEDGE) AND DIFFERENT SCHOOLS OF THOUGHT

Sunni Islam has different schools of thought, namely: Hanifites, Shafites, Malakites, Hanbalites, and Qadiani.

Hanifites

This is the school of Imam Abu Hanifa, who died in 767. Imam Abu Hanifa is one of the most prominent scholars of his time where he mostly relied on analogy. His followers are mostly in Afghanistan, Pakistan, India, Bangladesh, Iraq, and Egypt. He is buried in Iraq.

Malakites

This is the school of Imam Malik, who died in 795. His followers are mostly in Northern Africa. He is buried in Medina.

Shafites

This is the school of Imam Shafii, who died in 820. His followers are mainly in the gulf region of the Middle East. He is buried in Egypt.

Hanbalites

This is the school of Imam Ahmad Ibn Hanbal, who died in 855. His followers are mostly in the gulf region of Saudi Arabia. He is also buried in Iraq.

Qadiani

A branch of Sunni School of thought that believes Mirza Ghulam Ahmad is the Messiah. The majority of Muslims see them as heretics. Principally, they are located in Pakistan. However, they are spread worldwide and hold congregation as Muslims.

These four doctors of law, or Ulema, are highly respected within the Sunni branch of Islam. Each has their own interpretation and analogy based upon the Qur'an and the traditions of the Prophet. If they do not find anything in the Qur'an or the traditions, they have the intellectual power and ability to deliver a ruling called Fatwa, which Muslims in Sunni Islam accept and follow accordingly. Among these four Ulema, Imam Abu Hanifa strongly relied upon reason. He is considered to be the most liberal and flexible among the four Imams. These four figures made the Sharia (Law) more simple to understand and comprehendible to people. However, Muslim jurists continue exploring new analogies regarding what they face in contemporary life.

Shia Islam

The common denominator between Shia and Sunni Muslims is the belief in One God, the Prophet Mohammed as His last messenger and the Qur'an as the guide for humanity. After the era of the four righteous Caliphs, the difference of opinion between Shia and Sunni surfaced and divided them as two distinguished sects in Islam. Shia Muslims believe in the accession of Ali, the son-in-law of the Prophet, as the legitimate ruler of Muslims after the demise of the Prophet. They believe in Imamat- the chain of leadership should come through the family of the Prophet rather than the Ummah as the Sunnis believe. Shia Islam believes in the chains of Imams, starting from Ali, up to 12 Imams. The twelve Imams are as follows: first, Ali Ibn Abu Talib, the cousin and son-in-law of the Prophet. He was assassinated by his political foes in January of 661. Second, Imam Hassan Abu Mohammed Hassan Ibn Ali, known as Al Mujtaba (the chosen). He did not take a serious stand against Mu'awiya and secluded himself and retired in Medina. He led a quiet life and passed away at the early age of 46. Third, Imam Hussain, younger brother of Hassan. He is considered to be the third Imam in Shia Islam. His full name is Abu Abdullah Hussain Ibn Ali. After his martyrdom, he was given the title of Sayed Al Shuhadah (Prince of Martyrs). Imam Hussain did not sign the pledge of allegiance to Yazid, son of Mua'wiya, because he did not want to sign allegiance to a corrupt and drunkard person who was not qualified for khilafat at the plain of Karbala on October 680. Fourth, Imam Ali Zaynu'l- Abidin Abu Mohammed Ali Ibn Hussain, known as Zainu'l Abidin (the ornament of the worshippers), who died in 713. Fifth, Imam Mohammed Al Baqir Abu Jafar Mohammed Ibn Ali, known as Al Baqir (the ample in knowledge), who died in 740. Sixth, Imam Jafar Sidiq, known as Abu Abdullah Jafar Ibn Mohammed known as Sidiq (truthful), who died in 765. Seventh, Imam Musa Al Kazim, known as Abul Hassan Musa Ibn Jafar, known as Al Kazim (forbearing), who died in 799. Eighth, Ali Ar Ridha Abul Hassan Ali Ibn Musa, known as Ar Ridha (the approved or acceptable), who died in 818. Ninth, Imam Mohammed At Taqi Abu Jaffar Mohammed Ibn Ali, known as At Taqi (God Fearing), who died in 883. Tenth, Ali al Hadi Abul Hassan Ali Ibn Mohammed, known as Al Hadi (the guided), who died in 861.Eleventh, Imam Hassan Al Askari Abu Mohammed Hassan Ibn Ali, known as Al Askari (detention, due to his long life in Samaara), who died in 874. And twelfth, Imam Mohammed Al Mahdi, Abul Qasim Mohammed Ibn Hassan, known as Al Mahdi (the guided). Shia theologians believe that he has gone into occultation.   O C C U L T A T I O N

Imammat

Politically speaking, the main difference between the Sunni school of thought and the Shia school of thought is leadership of the Muslim community. Sunnis believe in Caliphat, while Shias believe in Imammat. A Caliph can be appointed by general consent of the people while an Imam comes from the Prophet's family one after another. The Imam, in Shia school of thought, is not only a political figure but is also a spiritual leader who leads the community and all affairs.

COMPILATION OF HADITH

After the Qur'an, the traditions of the Prophet of Islam are the main source of Islamic law. Hadiths, or sayings of the Prophet, and Sunnah, actions of the Prophet, are part of the laws of Islam. From a cultural anthropological standpoint, the traditions of the Prophet mold Islamic culture. One cannot have Islamic culture if he does not know the Hadiths of the Prophet. The Qur'an is guidance for humanity, but not, ethnologically and ethnographically speaking, a culture giver. For example, the Qur'an clearly states that Muslims must perform ritual prayers. But how, in what form, at what time, in what conditions that prayers must be performed comes from the Hadiths. Therefore, from a legal point of view, this is the second source of law, as well as anthropologically, the source of Islamic Culture.

The sayings of the Prophet were not collected during his lifetime. The reason for this was that the Prophet was apprehensive of people mixing verses of the Qur'an, coming from Allah, and his words, which was from his human mind, albeit by Divine inspiration. For this reason, he did not allow his words to be compiled during his lifetime. Nonetheless, his words and actions were memorized by his disciples. Long after his passing, it was decided that his words and actions should be collected. Thus, men of knowledge (ulema) worked very hard to collect his words and sayings. Since Hadiths were collected long after his passing, people deliberately made fake Hadiths. Thus, it was very hard for the Ulema to collect authentic Hadiths. However, with hard work, checking, cross checking, traveling, and researching, the Ulema managed to compile the Hadiths. Anthropologically speaking, this author categorized Hadiths on three principles. First, that Hadiths should relate and correspond directly to the Qur'an. For example, the Qur'an says: "Oh my Lord, advance me in knowledge." (Qur'an 20:114)[35] And, the Hadith follows with: (a) seek knowledge even in China, (b) from cradle to grave, seek knowledge, and (c) learning is mandatory for all men and women.

We can see that the above three Hadiths from the Prophet directly relate to the Qur'an, thus these Hadiths are all authentic. Second, before the advent of Islam, the Prophet of Islam was

---

[35] Qur'an 20:114

recorded as being trustworthy (Amin) by Muslims and non-Muslims. Thus, his personality was completely aloof from any sort of defect and wrong-doing, such as lying and cheating so a Hadith that does not correspond to the personality of the Prophet is not an authentic Hadith. Third, Islam came for social justice for all and all Hadiths must relate to justice. If it does not conform to justice, then it is not an authentic Hadith.

For the purpose of our research, we must also include the methods that the ulema compiled the Hadiths with and the sources of Hadiths for Muslims within the last 400 years. It is also important to note that there are disagreements about the authenticity of Hadiths between the Shia and Sunni sects of Islam. For example, temporary marriage is permissible in the Shia school of thought, while prohibited in the Sunni school of thought. This is because both schools view the historical background of the Hadiths differently.

The Centre for Peace and Spirituality is a great reference for the history of the compilation of Hadith. The following information can be found on their website, www.cpsglobal.org. The history of the compilation of Hadith may be broadly divided into four stages[36]:

> 1. The first stage relates to the period of the Prophet till 10 A.H.

> 2. The second stage is approximately from 11 A.H. to 100 A.H. This is the period of Sahaba, the Companions of the Prophet.

---

[36] http://www.cpsglobal.org/content/how-were-Hadith-compiled

3. The third stage is from about 101 to nearly 200 A.H. This is the period of the Tabiun, the disciples of the Companions of the Prophet.

4. The fourth stage is roughly from 200 A.H. to 300 A.H. This is the period of Taba Tabiun, the disciples of the disciples.

During the period of the Prophet and during the life of the Prophet, there was no regular compilation of the traditions for they were not generally recorded in writing. However, they were orally transmitted, with great accuracy of detail, thanks to the Arabs' exceptionally retentive memories.

1. Some companions had, however, prepared written collections of traditions for their own personal use. Those companions, in particular, who had weaker memories used to write them down for memorizing and preservation. These were also dictated to their disciples.

2. Then there were those companions who had administrative offices arranged for written copies of traditions, so that they might carry out their duties in the true spirit of Islam. For instance, while appointing Amr ibn Hazm as the governor of Yaman, the Prophet himself gave him a letter containing the times of prayer, methods of prayer, details of ablution, booty, taxation, zakat, etc.

3. Abdullah ibn Amr ibn al-As, a young Makkan, also used to write down all that he heard from the Prophet. He had even asked the Prophet if he could make notes of all that he said. The Prophet replied in the affirmative. Abdullah called this compilation Sahifah Sadiqa (The Book of the Truth). It was later incorporated into the larger collection of Imam Ahmad ibn Hanbal.

4. Anas, a young Madinan, was the Prophet's personal attendant. Since Anas remained with the Prophet day and night, he had greater opportunities than the other companions to listen to his words. Anas had written down the tradition on scrolls. He used to unroll these documents and say: "These are the sayings of the Prophet, which I have noted and then also read out to him to have any mistakes corrected."

5. Ali ibn Abi Talib was one of the scribes of the Prophet. The Prophet once dictated to him and he wrote on a large piece of parchment on both sides. He also had a sahifa (pamphlet) from the Prophet which was on zakat (the poor due) and taxes.

Besides these there were some other documents dictated by the Prophet himself — official letters, missionary letters, treaties of peace and alliance addressed to different tribes— all these were later incorporated into larger collections of Hadith.

After the death of the Prophet, interest in Hadith literature increased greatly on two accounts. Firstly, the Companions who knew the Hadith at first hand were gradually passing away. Their number continued to diminish day by day. Therefore, people became more keen to preserve the precious Hadith literature that had been stored in their memories. Secondly, the number of converts was growing and they showed great eagerness to learn as much about the traditions as possible.

This was the age of the rightly guided Caliphs. In this age the Companions had settled in almost all the countries conquered by the Muslims. People flocked to them to hear traditions from them. Thus a number of centers for the learning of traditions came into existence with these Companions as the focus. When a disciple had learned all the traditions he could from one Companion, he would go to the next Companion and so on, collecting as many traditions as possible. The zeal of these disciples was so great that they undertook long journeys to collect traditions from different Companions.

In this period, there were not many regular compilations. This was rather the period of collecting traditions. The work of compilation took place on a large scale during the age of Tabiun, the disciples of the disciples.

The Age of Tabiun from 101 to nearly 200 A.H.:

This is the age of the followers of the Companions of the Prophet. They devoted their entire lives to collecting traditions from different centers of learning, with the result that a large number of traditions were preserved. Now it became possible to collect several memoirs in larger volumes.

Mohd ibn Shihab Al Zuhri, the first regular compiler, was one of the most distinguished traditionists. Ibn Shihab Zuhri and Abu Bakr Al-Hazm were asked by Umar ibn Abdul Aziz, the Umayyad Caliph, to prepare a collection of all available traditions. Umar bin Abul Aziz wrote to Abu Bakr Al Hazm: "Whatever sayings of the Prophet can be found, write them down, for I fear the loss of knowledge and disappearance of learned men, and do not accept anything but the Hadith of the Holy Prophet, and people should make knowledge public."

The compilations made in this period do not exist today independently, having been incorporated into the larger collections of the later period. These collections were not exhaustive works on Hadith. Their nature was that of individual collections.

After the individual compilations of this period, comes the Al Muwatta of Imam Malik (716-795), the first regular work which contained a well-arranged collection of traditions. The number of the traditions collected by him is put at 1700. This came to be accepted as a standard work.

In this period the traditions respectively of the Prophet and his companions, and the decisions/edicts of the Tabiun were collected together in the same volume. However, it was mentioned with each narration whether it was that of the Prophet, his companions or of the followers.

The Third Age of Taba Tabiun (Followers of the Successors):

This age of the followers of the Companions' successors from 200 to 300 A.H., is the golden age in Hadith literature.

1. In this age the Prophet's traditions were separated from the reports of the Companions and their successors.

2. The authentic traditions were very carefully and painstakingly sifted from the "weak" traditions and then these were compiled in book-form.

3. Elaborate rules were framed, canons were devised to distinguish the true from the false traditions in accordance with clear principles.

The main attention of scholars who engaged themselves in the critical scrutiny of Hadith was given to the recorded chains of witnesses (isnad); whether the dates of birth and death and places of residence of witnesses in different generations were such as to have made it possible for them to meet, and whether they were trustworthy. This activity, to be properly carried out, involved some feeling for the authenticity of the text itself; an experienced traditionist would develop a sense of discrimination.

All traditions therefore fall into three general categories: (sahih) sound, having a reliable and uninterrupted isnad and a (matn) text that does not contradict orthodox belief; (hasan) good but those with an incomplete isnad or with transmitters of questionable authority; and (dhaif) weak those whose matn or transmitters are subject to serious criticism.

By the use of these criteria, the Hadith scholars were able to classify the traditions according to their degrees of reliability.

This is the period in which six authentic collections of traditions were compiled. These works are considered standard works on Hadith, and are known as the six correct books (sahih-e-sittah). The authors' names and book titles are as follows:

1. Mohammed b. Ismail al-Bukhari, (194 A.H.-256 A.H.): Sahih. This work is next to the Qur'an in authenticity according to Sunni scholars.

2. Muslim bin Qushairi (204 A.H.-261 A.H.): Sahih. This is the next most important work on Hadith according to Sunni scholars.

3. Ibn Majah (202 A.H.-275 A.H.): Sunan

4. Abu Isa al Tirmizi (209 A.H.-279 A.H.): Jame

5. Abu Abdur Rahman an Nasai (214 A.H.-303 A.H.): Sunan

6. Abu Da'ud (202 A.H.-275 A.H.): Sunan

The above was a chronology of Hadith according to the Center for Peace and Spirituality. This author also notes two things. Aisha, the Prophet's wife, was a great reporter of the Hadith. It is the opinion of this author that despite all efforts scholars made, contemporary research shows that there are either contradictory Hadiths in these volumes or mistaken Hadiths. For instance, one Hadith that contemporary research illuminated is regarding Aisha's age, reporting she was nine years old at the time of marriage, but consummated marriage at the age of thirteen. The research by Ansari, an Afghan scholar, shows that Aisha must have been between the ages of sixteen to nineteen when she married the Prophet. As a result of these mistakes in the Hadiths, millions of innocent young girls were married without their consent.

PART THREE

FUNDAMENTALS OF ISLAMIC CULTURAL ANTHROPOLOGY

ARTICLES OF FAITH

Muslims believe in six basic principles which are called Articles of Faith. First is the belief in Allah, who is the core of Islamic life. Second, belief in the Prophet Mohammed as the last messenger of Allah, and belief in passed Prophets of Allah who were before Mohammed and held the same message of Monotheism to humanity, such as Jesus, Moses, and Abraham (father of monotheism). Third, belief in previous scriptures that were given by God to other Prophets. Fourth, belief in Angels of Allah. These Angels have specific duties to fulfill with Allah's command. Fifth, belief in destiny, which means that despite the fact that humanity has been given freedom of choice, it does not control his life as to when he will die or what his lifetime will involve. Sixth, belief in the Hereafter; this means that every Muslim is accountable for what he does in this world. The significance of the Articles of Faith is to give Muslims a position of intellectuality, responsibility, identity, and direction so s/he exactly knows his/her place in history.

The following are the Articles of Faith as mentioned on the website Islamic Learning Materials[37]:

Belief in Allah –This belief requires Muslims to have the correct understanding and belief towards the Oneness of Allah. This concept is called Tawhid in Arabic. It is much more than just believing that Allah exists. It means believing that only He

---

[37] http://Islamiclearningmaterials.com/articles-of-faith-in-Islam/

deserves to be worshipped, and believing in His Divine Attributes. As explained earlier, Tawhid means Oneness of the whole universal system that Allah has created.

Beliefs in Prophethood of the Prophet as the last Messenger of Allah, and belief in all the Prophets before him, including Noah, Abraham, Moses and Jesus.

Belief in the Qur'an and the Books of Revelation with the Qur'an being the final word of God to humanity.

Belief in the Angels of God who transmit Allah's orders in His creation. According to Islam, they are created of light and their duty is to carry Allah's command only.

Belief in Destiny – This does not mean Muslims believe in fatalism. It means that there are certain things mankind does not have any control over, like when one departs from this life or when an Earthquake occurs.

Belief in the Day of Judgment – Believing in the Day of Judgment makes a person responsible to all he does in this life. According to Islam, people are raised after death to be accountable for all their actions.

99 ATTRIBUTES OF ALLAH

There are 99 attributes of Allah in the Qur'an, also called "names" of Allah. These attributes constitute a fundamental principle of Islamic cultural life in different ways. In mysticism, remembering and repeating these names over and over polish the heart. Spiritually, remembering these attributes remind one of the glory of the Creator and make him realize that He is the Creator, Protector, Provider, and Sustainer of the Universe. Intellectually, the attributes of Allah make a person realize his own social existence, that he is created by Allah who is the only source to be connected with for everything in life. The following are the 99 attributes of Allah:

Allah: He Who has the Godhood, which is the power to create entities.

1. Ar-Rahman: The One who is beneficent to both believers and blasphemers in this world, and especially for believers in the Hereafter.

2. Ar-Rahim: The One who has plenty of mercy for believers.

3. Al-Malik: The Peaceful One with complete Dominion, the One whose Dominion is clear from imperfection.

4. Al-Quddus: The One who is pure from any imperfection and clear from children and adversaries.

5. As-Salam: The Peaceful One who is free from every imperfection.

6. Al-Mu'min: The One who witnessed for Himself that no one is God but Him. And He witnessed for His believers that they are truthful in their beliefs, and no one is God but Him.

7. Al-Muhaymin: The One who witnesses the saying and deeds of His creatures.

8. Al-Aziz: The Defeater who is not defeated.

9. Al-Jabbar: The One where nothing happens in His Dominion, except which He willed.

10. Al-Mutakabbir: The One who is clear from the attributes of the creatures and from resembling them.

11. Al-Khaliq: The One who brings everything from non-existence to existence.

12. Al-Bari': The Creator who has the Power to turn entities.

13. Al-Musawwir: The One who forms His creatures in different pictures.

14. Al-Ghaffar: The One who forgives the sins of His slaves, time and time again.

15. Al-Qahhar: The Subduer who has the perfect Power and is not unable to do anything.

16. Al-Wahhab: The One who is Generous in giving plenty without any return.

17. Ar-Razzaq: The One who gives everything that benefits, whether Halal or Haram.

18. Al-Fattah: The One who opens for His slaves closed worldly and religious matters.

19. Al-Alim: The Knowledgeable; the One for whom nothing is absent from His knowledge.

20. Al-Qabid and 21. Al-Basit: The One who constricts the sustenance of His wisdom and expands and widens with His Generosity and Mercy.

22. Al-Khafid and 23. Ar-Rafi: The One who lowers whomever He wills by His Destruction and raises whomever He wills by His Endowment.

24. Al-Muziz and 25. Al-Muthil: He gives esteem to whomever He wills, hence there is no one to degrade Him; And He degrades whomever He wills, hence, there is no one to give Him esteem.

26. As-Sami: The One who Hears all things that are heard by His Eternal Hearing without an ear, instrument, or organ.

27. Al-Basir: The One who Sees all things that are seen by His Eternal Seeing without a pupil or any other instrument.

28. Al-Hakam: He is the Ruler and His judgment is His Word.

29. Al-Adl: The Just One who is entitled to do what He does.

30. Al-Latif: The One who is kind to His slaves and endows upon them.

31. Al-Khabir: The One who knows the truth of things.

32. Al-Halim: The One who delays punishment for those who deserve it and He might then forgive them.

33. Al-Azim: The One deserving the attributes of Exaltment, Glory, Extolment, and Purity from all imperfection.

34. Al-Ghafur: The One who forgives a lot.

35. Ash-Shakur: The One who gives a lot of reward for little obedience.

36. Al-Aliyy: The One who is clear from the attributes of the creatures.

37. Al-Kabir: The One who is greater than everything in status.

38. Al-Hafiz: The One who protects whatever and whomever He wills to protect.

39. Al-Muqit: The One who has the Power.

40. Al-Hasib: The One who gives the satisfaction.

41. Aj-Jalil: The One who is attributed with greatness of Power and Glory of status.

42. Al-Karim: The One who is clear from abjectness.

43. Ar-Raqib: The One that nothing is absent from Him. Hence, its meaning is related to the attribute of Knowledge.

44. Al-Mujib: The One who answers the one in need if he asks Him and rescues the yearner if he calls upon Him.

45. Al-Wasi: The Knowledgeable.

46. Al-Hakim: The Wise One who is correct in His doings.

47. Al-Wadud: The One who loves His believing slaves and His believing slaves love Him. His love to His slaves is His Will to be merciful to them and praise them. Hence, its meaning is by which He related to the attributes of the Will and Kalam (His attribute with which He orders and forbids and spoke to Mohammed and Musa. It is not a sound, nor a language, nor a letter).

48. Al-Majeed: The Glorious One who is with perfect Power, High Status, Compassion, Generosity and Kindness.

49. Al-Baith: The One who resurrects His slaves after death for reward and/or punishment.

50. Ash-Shahid: The One who nothing is absent from Him.

51. Al-Haqq: The One who truly exists.

52. Al-Wakil: The One who gives the satisfaction and is relied upon.

53. Al-Qawiyy: The One with the complete Power.

54. Al-Matin: The One with extreme Power, which is uninterrupted, and He does not get tired.

55. Al-Waliyy: The Supporter.

56. Al-Hamid: The praised One who deserves to be praised.

57. Al-Muhsi: The One who the count of things are known to him.

58. Al-Mubdi': The One who started the human being. That is, He created him.

59. Al-Muid: The Restoring who brings back the creatures after death.

60. Al-Muhyi: The One who took out a living human from semen that does not have a soul. He gives life by giving the souls back to the worn out bodies on the resurrection day and He makes the hearts alive by the light of knowledge.

61. Al-Mumit: The One who renders the living dead.

62. Al-Hayy: The One attributed with a life that is unlike our life and is not that of a combination of soul, flesh or blood.

63. Al-Qayyum: The One who remains and does not end.

64. Al-Wajid: The Rich who is never poor. Al-Wajd is Richness.

65. Al-Wahid: The One without a partner.

66. Al-Majid: The All Noble One.

67. Al-Ahad: The Sole One

68. As-Samad: The Master who is relied upon in matters and reverted to in ones needs.

69. Al-Qadir: The One attributed with Power.

70. Al-Muqtadir: The One with the perfect Power that nothing is withheld from Him.

71. Al-Muqaddim and 72. Al-Mu'akhkhir: The One who puts things in their right places. He makes ahead what He wills and delays what He wills.

73. Al-Awwal: The One whose Existence is without a beginning.

74. Al-'Akhir: The One whose Existence is without an end.

75. Az-Zahir and 76. Al-Batin: The One that nothing is above Him and nothing is underneath Him, hence, He exists without a place. He, The Exalted, His Existence is obvious by proofs and He is clear from the delusions of attributes of bodies.

77. Al-Wali: The One who owns things and manages them.

78. Al-Mutaali: The One who is clear from the attributes of the creation.

79. Al-Barr: The One who is kind to His creatures, who covered them with His sustenance and willed among them by His support, protection, and special mercy.

80. At-Tawwab: The One who grants repentance to whomever He willed among His creatures and accepts his repentance.

81. Al-Muntaqim: The One who victoriously prevails over His enemies and punishes them for their sins. It may mean the One who destroys them.

82. Al-Afuww: The One with wide forgiveness.

83. Ar-Ra'uf: The One with extreme Mercy. The Mercy of Allah is His will to endow upon whomever He willed among His creatures.

84. Malik Al-Mulk: The One who controls the Dominion and gives dominion to whomever He willed.

85. Thul-Jalal wal-Ikram: The One who deserves to be Exalted and not denied.

86. Al-Muqsit: The One who is Just in His judgment.

87. Aj-Jami: The One who gathers the creatures on a day that there is no doubt about, that is the Day of Judgment.

88. Al-Ghaniyy: The One who does not need the creation.

89. Al-Mughni: The One who satisfies the necessities of the creatures.

90. Al-Mani: The Supporter who protects and gives victory to His pious believers. Al-Mu'tiy The Withholder

91. Ad-Darr and 92. An-Nafi: The One who makes harm reach to whomever He willed and benefit to whomever He willed.

93. An-Nur: The One who guides.

94. Al-Hadi: The One whom with His Guidance His believers were guided, and with His Guidance the living: beings have been guided to what is beneficial for them and protected from what is harmful to them.

95. Al-Badi: The One who created the creation and formed it without any preceding example.

96. Al-Baqi: The One that the state of non-existence is impossible for Him.

97. Al-Warith: The One whose Existence remains.

98. Ar-Rashid: The One who guides.

99. As-Sabur: The One who does not quickly punish the sinners.

The Qur'an refers to these 99 names in the following verse: "God! There is no God but Him! To Him belong the most excellent names."(Qur'an 20:8)[38] And, also: "Say to the people, O Prophet: Call upon God, or Call upon the All- Merciful. By either name you may call Him. For He is One and to Him alone belong the most excellent names." (Qur'an 17:110)[39]

---

[38] Qur'an 20:8
[39] Qur'an 17:110

It is believed that Allah has one hundred names or attributes, but 99 of them are known to the ordinary person. Out of the 99 attributes, four are not to be used as people's names, and are: Al-Mutakabbir, Al-Qahhar, Al-Qabid, and Al-Khafid. Because these are only Allah's attributes, they cannot be implied directly to a child. So, many of these attributes are used as names in families with a prefix and these prefixes detach the attributes from humankind. For example, Al Rahman is an attribute of Allah and to use it as a proper name, Muslims add the prefix "Abd" pronouncing it as Abdul Rahman. Abdul means slave of and so Abdul Rahman means Slave of God. Or, the attribution of Allah is Al Noor, and to use it as a proper name for an individual, Muslims add the suffix at the end of Noor such as Din and that would be Noor Udin, which means Light of Din. Since Monotheism teaches oneness of God, the 99 attributes stand as an odd number because God is One. Most prayer beads (Muslim Rosary) are either 33 in count or 99 in count because these two numbers are odd numbers. Thus, one cannot have prayer beads that count with even numbers because that is against the culture of Monotheism.

FIVE PILLARS OF ISLAM

The five pillars of Islam are extremely important anthropologically, because not only do they make a person enter the faith, but they mold him culturally. The five pillars, as they are usually called, change a person's mentality about his own social existence, his vision for a universal system, his world view on history and, most importantly, accepting the universal system as one whole body, which is the *Tawhid*. Therefore, the five pillars of Islam are not a religious ritual, rather a composition of human life in existence and his relationship to the universe and his Creator.

SHAHADA (DECLARATION OF FAITH)

The five pillars begin with the Declaration of Faith. The five pillars are the building blocks of a monument or building that make it stand. Declaration of Faith is a statement that one utters by tongue and wholeheartedly believes in it. If one does not believe by heart, he cannot be a Muslim. The Declaration of Faith opens the door to accepting God and Mohammed as his Prophet, which states: "La ilaha illalah, Mohammad rasoolillah," which means there is no god but God, and Mohammed is His messenger. The Declaration of Faith also positions human beings as natural beings and makes them join the universal law, where the law of nature and the law of God are one and the same. Mankind is part of the natural system and the natural system is part of mankind. Shahada means witness. A person witnesses the truthfulness of God and his Prophet. When a person makes the profession of faith, theologically, he becomes a Muslim, but, philosophically, he submits to the law of nature which has been created by God. This is because Islam means submission to the will of God. The will of God in this respect is His creation. Mankind accepts this creation and sees himself within it. Declaration of Faith has two parts which can be read in one sentence. The first part is there is no god but God. It means that God of the universe is the only One and He is the Creator, Protector, Sustainer and Law-giver of the universal system. This statement of there is no god but God directly places emphasis on *Tawhid,* in which God is the ruler of the universe and mankind. However, He grants mankind the freedom to conduct his life based upon His guidance. Hence, if man is responsible for his own destiny, then *Tawhid* rejects theocracy. This is the beauty of *Tawhid*, where man has been given freedom of choice and, at the same time, cannot detach himself from the universal law that God designed for human understanding, felicity, and achievement. The second part of the Declaration of Faith, Mohammed is the Messenger, encompasses not only accepting his Prophethood, but also his leadership in the community of nations. The declaration of both parts of the faith creates the legal principle of the Islamic judicial system, which is justice for all, as the Qur'an states: "And when you judge between a man and a man, that you judge with justice." (Qur'an 4; 58)[40] According to Islamic Cultural Anthropology, Declaration of Faith grants humanity a principle of social existence, a civilized way of life, and distinguishes humanity from the animal kingdom, vegetation kingdom, and other creations. Declaration of Faith grants humanity responsibility, along with dignity and integrity as the Creator's successor on Earth. Declaration of Faith grants humanity direction, objectives, and goals that, if followed properly, one will not be lost nor stray from the universal principle as a natural being. Declaration of Faith also acknowledges and recognizes a human being's role within the universal system. Theologically, it makes one a Muslim when he accepts God as his sovereign and Mohammed as his Prophet, and obeys both.

SALAH (RITUAL DAILY PRAYER)

Prayer is the second pillar of Islam, and after the Declaration of Faith, is the most important pillar in Islam. A

---

[40] Qur'an 4:58

human being is a hylomorphic entity, meaning that a human being is made of corpse and spirit. God created humanity with His own spirit and He says in the Qur'an: "Then He proportioned him and breathed into him from His [created] soul and made for you hearing and vision and hearts; little are you grateful." (Qur'an 32:9)[41] This verse clearly indicates that Allah's spirit is with human beings and thus, human beings are never alone. Prayer in Islam is not merely meditation. Prayer has three meanings. The first is people offer supplications. The second meaning of Salah (prayer) is connection. It is through prayer that a human being can connect himself to the source of knowledge and wisdom. This way, man can be inspired to lead his life with wisdom and understanding of his own-self and the whole creation. Prayer in Islam is like a light in the mind of an individual. Just how a light illuminates a room or a house; prayer illuminates the mind and spirit of a human being. It is through this connection, illumination, and going to the source of knowledge that mankind not only maintains a balance and stays away from corruption, but also makes a person aware of where he comes from and where he ends up. Prayer energizes a human being to achieve his goal and reach his maximum potential. Scientifically, prayer helps to be stress free and work, act and perform normally. The third meaning of prayer, or Salah, is to cleanse. This means that in each prayer a person revitalizes his energy and reenergizes his potential to achieve his desired goals. In this respect, these goals are not only worldly goals, but also to secure the world of Hereafter, free of sin and to join God. It is impossible for people to not make a mistake daily when challenged by daily routines. These small mistakes can be washed away through prayer. Steadfast prayer, according to the Qur'an, makes people prosper, which means that through prayer mankind not only accepts God as his ruler and law giver, but

---

[41] Qur'an 32:9

acknowledges that he comes from Him and returns to Him. One symbolic meaning of prostration is that one returns to Him. At the same time, prayer gains mankind prosperity in the Hereafter. The idea of prayer is that mankind needs his Creator for all his life perspectives, according to Islam. And prayer, when established properly, moves a human being closer to his Creator and this closeness defeats forces of evil. Prayer becomes a defense and protection against all evils. The Qur'an states: "But bow down in adoration and bring yourself closer to Allah."(Qur'an 96; 19)[42] On the other hand, those who lose this connection with God, will float without purpose, objective, and goals in life, and there is no being to protect them and that is his loss. "So woe to the worshippers who are neglectful of their prayers."(Qur'an 107; 4 and 5)[43] From a cultural point of view, according to a Hadith of the Prophet Mohammed, the difference between a Muslim and a non-Muslim is prayer. Theologically, prayer is mandatory for all men. However, it is restricted for women due to feminine excuses. There are three kinds of prayer in Islam: mandatory prayers (fard), the Sunnah of the Prophet, and optional prayers. First, mandatory prayers are to be performed five times at dawn, noon, afternoon, sunset, and evening. Prayers are different in length. Mandatory prayers are those that are mandatory by God and a Muslim must perform without exception. All mandatory prayers are joined by traditional prayers, which are called Sunnah prayers, that are performed either before or after the mandatory prayer. Dawn prayer is four rakat (the number of compulsory recitations of the opening chapter of the Qur'an (while standing) or the unit of the number of bows in each prayer), two mandatory and two Sunnah, which should be performed before the mandatory. Noon prayer is ten rakat, four Sunnah, four mandatory and two

---

[42] Qur'an 96:19
[43] Qur'an 107:4 and 5

Sunnah. Afternoon is four rakat mandatory. Sunset is five rakat, which is three mandatory, plus two Sunnah. Evening prayer is six rakat, four mandatory and two Sunnah. In some schools of thought, such as Hanafi, there are three additional, optional prayers at night, which are called *witr*. Traditional prayers, called Sunnah prayers, are those prayers that the Prophet of Islam prayed regularly after or before mandatory prayers. In some schools of thought it became part of the daily regular prayers while optional prayers are those prayers that people pray when they desire. It should be noted that optional prayers are all traditions of the Prophet of Islam. However, people are not obligated to perform optional prayers if they do not desire to do so. Examples include prayer before traveling, prayer upon arriving back home, or prayer for rain. Prayer cannot be accepted without ablution (wudu). There are three kinds of ablutions. One is ghusul, a washing of the whole body (compulsory) and highly recommended before Friday prayers. Second is asghar, the lesser ablution, which a Muslim performs by washing his hands to the elbow, face and massaging head with wet fingers, and washing feet. A third ablution is dry wudu (tayamum). This is when a Muslim does not have access to water, thus, he makes the intention of wudu and wipes his face and hands with clean dry dust that purifies him to perform prayer.

Characteristics & Rituals of Performing Prayer

Wudu (Ablution)

In Islam, every religious performance has physical, as well as spiritual, applications or significance. Ablution is a command by God in the Qur'an that people should perform before standing for ritual prayers. A ritual prayer will not be accepted without cleaning oneself. *Tahaara* (cleansing) has two aspects: Tahaara, cleansing of the heart and cleansing of the body. Both of them, the heart and the body, are interrelated. One has to work hard to clean his heart by remembrance of God

(Zikr), avoid gossiping, back biting, ill-thinking of others, and shun away from jealousy. And to improve the soul and heart for a better life, one has to contribute to society, reconcile people with one another, and propagate Islam with modesty and good words, stay away from violence, corruption, bribery, and hypocrisy. It is through these performances and achievements of the soul that one reaches felicity. Washing of the body has two parts. One is ablution, which involves washing the arm to the elbow, washing the mouth, washing the face and massaging the scalp and washing the feet. After, one is ready to stand before God and perform his ritual prayers. Ablution is a form of worship. Every performance that is recommended by God is an act of worship. Ablution not only cleanses someone physically, but revitalizes and reenergizes him to stand before God for worship in a fresh state of mind. There are three types of ablution. The greater ablution is called the Ghusul, the second type is the lesser, called Wudu Asghar, and the third type is dry ablution, called Tayammum. When a married couple approaches one another sexually and commits the act of intercourse, a Ghusul (taking a full bath) is required. It is also recommended by the Prophet that a Ghusul can be delayed, but must be taken before standing for prayers. However, a couple must wash their private parts immediately after the act of intercourse. In case water is not available, Tayammum is required. One has to find clean dust and touch the dust lightly and rub his face and arms with it. Every ablution must begin with the Niah (intention) that states: "I intend to take this ablution to purify myself and make ready myself for prayers." After the ablution is over, one must recite the following:

"Allahumma aj alni Minal tawabeena
wa minal mutatahireen."

"Oh my lord accept my repentance
And accept my ablution."

When entering the bathroom one has to recite the following invocation:

"Allahuma inee awudhu beka
minal khobse wal khabayes"

"Oh Allah I seek refuge with from all
Offensive and wicked things
(Evil deeds and evil spirits)."

Adhan (Call for prayer)

Adhan is the call for prayer. A male person will stand and call for ritual prayers for people to join in the prayer. It reads as:

"Allaahu Akbar (God is Great),
Allaahu Akbar (God is Great),
Allaahu Akbar (God is Great),
Allaahu Akbar (God is Great),
Ashhadu Allah ilaaha illa-Lah (I bear witness that there is no other god but God),
Ashhadu Allah ilaaha illa-Lah (I bear witness that there is no other god but God),
Ash Hadu anna Muhamadar rasuulullah (I bear witness that Mohammed is the messenger of God),
Ash Hadu anna Muhamadar rasuulullah (I bear witness that Mohammed is the messenger of God), Hayya' alas Salaah (Come to Prayer),
Hayya' alas Salaah (Come to Prayer),
Hayya' ala Falaah (Come to Success),
Hayya' ala Falaah (Come to Success),
Allaahu Akbar (God is Great) ,
Allaahu Akbar (God is Great),
Laa ilaaha illa-Lah (There is no god but God)".

People should recite the following invocation when they hear the call for prayer:

"O Allah! Lord of this perfect call (of not ascribing partners to you) and of the regular prayer which is going to be established! Kindly give Mohammed the right of intercession and superiority and send him (on the Day of Judgment) to the best and the highest place in Paradise which You promised him); then intercession for me will be permitted for him on the Day of Resurrection"). (Volume 1. Page 339 Hadith 588, Sahih Bukhari)[44]

When one focuses on the meaning of the Adhan (call for ritual prayers), it is obvious that it is not only looking to the meaning of Adhan, a call for prayer for people to assemble, but also an awakening of the heart and mind for the sake of faith in which they have in their hearts. Looking to the meaning of Adhan, which states: "come to success," tells us that the call is not merely like ringing a bell or blowing a horn as the Jews used to do, or clapping as the Christians used to do, but is more like inviting people to the faith, because, according to Islam, it is only faith (Iman) that makes a person succeed. Therefore, Adhan, by its own nature, has a spiritual application and meaning in the life of a Muslim. Also, when the call for prayer is called, it connects an individual to his or her source in which that is God. That means by accepting the call for prayer and attending prayer, he finds his position as a human being universally. He knows that he has more responsibilities in his daily prayers. There are some ritual prayers, such as Eid prayers or funeral prayers, where there is no Adhan required. Adhan is only required for the five daily ritual prayers and Friday prayers. On Fridays, the call for prayer occurs twice; once when the prayer is due and a second time when the Imam stands to give the sermon.

---

[44] Volume 1. Page 339 Hadith 588, Sahih Bukhari

Qibla (Direction of prayer)

Qibla is the direction that Muslims face when engaged in ritual prayer. In Muslim religious practice, worshippers must turn to face one single direction during daily prayers. The Qibla is the direction of the Ka'aba in Mecca, in modern-day Saudi Arabia. When possible, mosques are constructed in such a way that one side of the building faces the Qibla, making it easier to organize worshippers into rows for prayer. The direction of the Qibla is also often marked in the front of the mosque with an ornamental indentation in the wall, known as a mihrab. It should be noted that Muslims do not worship the Ka'aba. The Ka'aba is the capital and focal point of the entire Muslim world. The Qur'an states: "And from wherever you go out (for prayer), turn your face toward al-Masjid al-Haram. And wherever you (believers) may be, turn your faces toward it in order that people will not have any argument against you, except for those of them who commit wrong; so fear them not but fear Me. And (it is) so I may complete My favor upon you and that you may be guided." (Qur'an 2:150)[45] This direction of Ka'aba is not designated for only the people around Ka'aba, but the entire world and the word Shattar al Masjid means that wherever one is in the world in any corner, they must face Ka'aba. The word Shattar designates the direction all around the world towards Ka'aba. It is extremely important to note that not only is the Ka'aba the focal point of unity for Muslims, but the direction of Ka'aba for prayer all around the world unites people for the same cause and the same objective.

Cleanliness of a Prayer Place

One condition of performing prayers is to perform in a clean area, away from unsanitary areas. Also, the spot where one performs must be very clean, and that is why Muslims have prayer rugs. Prayer rugs are not used for any other purpose but for prayers. The third condition is the clothing one wears during prayer must be spotless and clean. It is recommended, especially

---

[45] Qur'an 2:150

for Friday Prayers, that people wear their most beautiful garments and wear perfume. Muslims must remember, according to Prophet Mohammad, cleanliness is half of the faith.

Mosque

Mosque (masjid) is not only a place of worship, but also the center for Muslim gatherings and learning. A Mosque plays a major role in the history of Islam. The Prophet of Islam not only gave sermons in the mosque, but also guided people towards the right path, educated people, taught people, and issued economic and political decrees. In the mosque, people used to sit and exchange ideas on knowledge and learning. During ritual prayers in the mosque, men stand in front and women stand behind, and when prayer is over, men are to wait until all women have left and then may leave the mosque. People are not allowed to litter or raise their voices in the mosque. One must park his vehicle further away if there is no parking available, and walk to the mosque. It should be noted that the mosque is a place for worship, however, Muslims can pray anywhere as long as they have ablution and a clean area. No ground is holy and not consecrated.

I'tikaaf

Itikaaf is a spiritual practice that people may perform in the last ten days of Ramadan. During the last ten days, both men and women stay in the mosque and go into deep spiritual training by performing prayer, *Zikr* (remembering of Allah), and avoiding sexual intercourse or relations with wives and husbands. The Qur'an states: "But do not ever lie with them for so long as you may be in ritual retreat in the mosques of God." (Qur'an 2:187)[46] This is not a mandatory religious command, but optional. People may leave the mosque for special needs, like

---

[46] Qur'an 2:187

taking ablution or washing one's body and changing clothes or visiting the sick (while remaining standing), but nothing more if they commit to this special ritual retreat.

Mandatory and Optional Prayers

The Qur'an says, "And keep up the prayer and bring the zakat and bow down with the ones bowing down."(Qur'an 2:43)[47] After the Declaration of Faith in Islam, ritual prayer is mandatory daily five times for all Muslim adults. The Prophet Mohammed required parents to teach their children the performance and daily prayers starting at the age of seven. Rejecting prayers intentionally is infidelity, and not performing but accepting it as the truth, is a sin. Prayer, called Salaat in the Qur'an, has three meanings. One is ritual daily prayers, second is a connection that means with prayer he connects with his Creator who is the source of knowledge, mercy and forgiveness. It is by performing prayers that man has the ability and opportunity to connect to the source and ask for guidance and protection. Third, Salaat also means to burn. So every time one stands for prayer, he burns his minor sins by performing prayers for whatever wrong doing he has done or mistakes that he has committed. And every time one performs prayers, one has the opportunity to purify his soul and revitalize his energy and move forward for a better living. It is widely believed among Muslims that prayers clean the soul, and that is why it is mandatory to keep a person always in a state of purity. Prayers will keep people away from wrongdoing and corruption. Of course it is understandable that those who pray, but commit wrongdoings, such as committing robbery, violating people's rights and lying and cheating, simply did not understand and comprehend the meaning and significance of his prayers. The meanings of prayers posture a believer to stand in front of his lord in the most humble way and

---

[47] Qur'an 2:43

declare: "Allahu Akbar" addressing the fact that He is Great. In fact, standing and saying "Allahu Akbar" is a form of salutation to Almighty God. Bowing means that a believer only bows to his Sustainer, Protector, Provider and Creator. This posture gives a person dignity and integrity. He is not to bow to any being like kings or people of power, but only to his Creator. Kneeling and touching the forehead on the ground means that a Muslim admits in front of his Lord that he is made of dust and will return and become dust. After finishing ritual prayers, the believer says peace to both of his sides, both right and left hand; and those greetings are for the Angels that accompany him all his life, and according to Islamic theology, his deeds will be recorded daily.

Mandatory Prayers

Origin of Five Daily Prayers

According to Peer (spiritual master) of the Path Abdullah Ansari, the first who performed morning ritual prayers was Adam. It was he who was redeemed from the darkness of night to the lightness of day. Because of this gift from Allah, he prayed two rakat in the morning. Adam had not seen the night, and was away from his partner and suddenly saw himself miserable at night and thus communicated with Allah. When it became dawn, he was commanded to perform two rakat for the passing of the night, the coming of the day, and for seeing his companion.

The first person who performed noon prayer was Abraham, the Father of Monotheism. Because he obeyed and attempted to sacrifice his son for the sake of Allah, and his attempt for sacrifice was accepted by Allah, he was called to perform four rakat for the following four reasons: one, to be thankful for success; second, to be thankful for affirmation or confirmation of the truth; third, to be thankful for the call; and fourth, to be thankful for sacrifice.

The first person who performed afternoon prayer (Asr) was the Prophet Yunus. Because he left the preaching of his people, he was overcome by a fish and after forgiveness, was released from the fish and saw himself out of darkness for the following four reasons: the darkness of shortcoming, the darkness of the night, the darkness of water and escape from the darkness of the womb of the fish. He was called to pray four rakat.

The first person who performed sunset prayer was the Prophet Jesus, who came to this world without a father. While he was in his mother's womb, he was taught Torah and Gospel and spoke in the cradle. Because of these three gifts and blessings from God, he performed three rakat. The first rakat was because he disclaimed being God, the second rakat is proof of Allah for the two monotheistic books, and the third rakat he performed was for the Oneness of God.

The first person who performed night prayer was the Prophet Moses. When he was thinking about the homeland, night arrived and a big wind was blown, rain poured, thunder was striking and he had four senses of grief. The grief of his wife and child, the grief of his brother and the grief of the enemy; he was called: "Don't worry I'm the one who relieved you from grief!" and Moses stood and prayed four rakat for that gift from God.

Procedure and Timing of the Five Daily Prayers

Morning prayer is before sunrise (Fajr prayer) and consists of two rakat. A rakat is a cycle of ritual actions and phrases coming from the traditions of the Prophet Mohammed, and the phrases are from the verses of the Qur'an. Each ritual prayer and each rakat begins with Al Fatiha, which is the first chapter of the Qur'an. Al Fatiha is called "The Key to Paradise". Noon prayer (Zuhr) is four rakat and afternoon prayer (Asr) is also four rakat. Sunset prayer (Maghrib) consists of three rakat and night prayer (Isha) consists of four rakat. It is important to note that congregation prayer in Islam has more rewards than praying by oneself. Thus, this encourages people to go to the mosque and join the congregation, or even at home a family should stand together at the time of prayer and pray together. The Prophet of Islam stated: "That prayer in congregation is 27 times more superior to prayer offered by one person alone." It is extremely important that the ritual five times daily prayers are performed during a specified time according to the Qur'an, and the Qur'an states: "Verily, the prayer is enjoined on the believers at fixed hours." (Qur'an 4:103)[48] This fixed time applies only to five times daily prayers as mentioned earlier. Here, the Qur'an connects human beings to the universal system as part of a natural entity. Again, the law of nature and law of Allah is one and the same. The reason fixed times are important is because it relates to the sun and rotation of the Earth. For example, the morning prayer is before sunrise, noon prayer is when the sun is shifting along the meridian, and the evening prayer is at sunset.

Friday Prayer

Congregational Friday prayer is mandatory for all Muslim male adults who are residing in a city or a town. However, women may attend if they wish, but should not pray if they have feminine excuses. Children are encouraged, but not mandated to. Friday is a day of festival for Muslims. According to the saying of the Prophet: "the world has been created on Friday and will be destroyed on Friday." Also, it is said that Adam and Eve were created on Friday. Thus, Friday is not a Sabbath day; people ay go to Friday prayer and then return to work. Theologically, there is no day of rest in Islam; however, in Islamic countries, Friday prayers are usually performed mid-

---

[48] Qur'an 4:103

day. Therefore, Friday is a day of rest for Islamic countries; people have the day off and enjoy time with family. Friday prayer is mandatory according to the Qur'an, as it states: "O you who believe when the call to congregation is made on Friday, then proceed at once to the remembrance of God and the prayer, and quit all commerce, this is best for you, if only you were to know Gods reward for it. But when the prayers are concluded, then you may flee freely throughout the land and seek out the bounty of God." (Qur'an 62: 9 and 10)[49]

Traditions of Friday Prayers

From a cultural and anthropological point of view, Friday prayer has rules and regulations that one has to follow. One, take a bath, men trim their beards, change into clean clothes, put on perfume, not eat before prayer, and brush teeth with Sawak (a plant that smells good and cleans teeth). The Prophet used to use Sawak before Friday prayer. If Sawak is not available, then Muslims should continue to brush their teeth and rinse their mouths. The reason is that mouths should not smell of food and one should not be heavy when praying. Two, go to the mosque as early as possible. Three, upon entering the mosque, perform two rakat of prayers, called *Tahya,* which means being grateful for the mosque. Four, sit quietly; either do zikr (remembrance of God), or recite the Qur'an quietly. Five, after the first call for prayer, perform four rakat of Sunnah, then wait for the second call for prayer. Six, after the second call for prayer, the Imam stands and recites the Khutba (sermon) and believers should attentively listen, learn, and not speak. Seven, after the Khutba, the two rakat prayers begin and one should stand beside others humbly, shoulder to shoulder, toe to toe, and without any gap in between. Eight, after prayer, there is a great

---

[49] Qur'an 62:9 and 10

reward if one performs four more rakat, then greets everyone and leaves the mosque with the left foot, to uphold the Sunnah of the Prophet. It should be mentioned that if someone arrives late to the mosque, he is not to make his way to the front and disrupt others but quietly and peacefully, pray two rakats, and take a seat where available.

Optional Prayers

Sunnah prayers are traditional prayers that the Prophet Mohammed performed in addition to mandatory prayers. These prayers are called Sunnah prayers or Nafil prayers. However, there is a slight difference between Sunnah prayers and Nafil prayers. Sunnah prayers are those that are either performed before mandatory prayers or after prayers. They are a total of twelve rakats. Prophet Mohammed stated: "A house will be built in paradise for anyone who prays day and night twelve rakat." These twelve rakats are divided as follows: two rakat before dawn prayers, four rakat before noon prayer, two rakat during afternoon prayer, two rakats after the sunset prayer and two rakats during the night prayer, which makes a total of twelve rakats according to the Prophet Mohammed's Hadith. There are no Sunnah prayers for the afternoon. Sunnah prayers are not mandatory and it is not a sin not to perform them. If they do perform them, they gain a greater reward from their Lord. However, among the twelve rakat of Sunnah prayers, there are some that are highly emphasized by the Prophet and have high rewards, especially the two rakat before the dawn prayer and the two rakat after the sunset prayer. This is because during the five times daily prayer, the dawn prayer and the sunset prayer are extremely important. As the Qur'an mentions: "Be ever steadfast in observing the prayer at the declining of the sun, until the darkening of the night. Moreover, hold fast to the Qur'ans recitation at the dawn Prayer. Indeed, the recitation at dawn is ever witnessed by hosts of angels and believers."(Qur'an

17:78)[50] This does not mean the other three prayers are not important, however since the Qur'an mentions the two ends of the day, it has more weight because of the Qur'an's references. From a cultural and anthropological point of view, it is more important to note that anything from the Qur'an, such as the above verse, has a preference theologically. Those injunctions from the Qur'an have a preference over the Hadith, which comes after the Qur'an.

Nafil Prayers

Nafil prayers are optional prayers that one can perform anytime. The two nafil prayers mentioned are very common among Muslims, and one of them is performed after two rakat during the night prayer, called Witr. Witr is three rakat and is separate from the prescribed mandatory prayers, and Sunnah prayers. Since the Prophet performed it daily, it has also become a Sunnah of the Prophet (a tradition of the Prophet). Another nafil prayer is *Tahajud,* according to the Hadith of the Prophet, it is a prayer that people wake after midnight and before dawn for and perform, typically eight rakat, plus three witr at the end. There are more rewards with this prayer when Muslims prolong prostrations during this prayer.

Fear Prayer

This is a prayer that is performed when a person fears his enemies. It is the only prayer that can be performed standing or riding to ask Allah for help and victory.

Rain Wishing Prayer

Rain wishing prayers were performed by the Prophet when rain was needed. Today, people ask their Imam to lead them in performing rain wishing prayers.

---

[50] Qur'an 17:78

Eclipse Prayer

It was the tradition of the Prophet of Islam that when the sun and moon eclipse, the Prophet prayed two rakat prayers and mentioned that the eclipse was a sign of Allah, and we have to pray until it passes. It is also recommended that after prayers, people give charity. Eclipse prayers can be performed individually or in congregation. If it is in congregation, a short sermon is recommended.

Tarawih Prayer

Tarawih is one of the Nafil prayers that has great reward in the month of Ramadan and consists of praying at night during Ramadan. It is not a mandatory prayer, so people are not obliged to pray every night. It has been reported that the Prophet had stated that whomever prayed at night during the month of Ramadan, out of sincere faith and hoping for a reward from Allah, then all of his previous sins would be forgiven. People can perform this prayer individually or collectively as a congregation. Nowadays, it is mostly held as a congregation in the mosque where the Imam recites the Qur'an in a sequence for the entire month. Since there is no specific ruling in this matter, some congregations finish before the month of Ramadan ends. For example, they can finish in 15 days or 21 days. It depends upon how many chapters of the Qur'an are being recited. However, according to the Hadith of the Prophet, if one wants to receive the reward, he should pray this optional prayer every night until the end of Ramadan.

Traveling Prayer

When Muslims leave their homes for a destination, and travel is required, they should perform prayer and ask Allah to grant them a safe trip. This is performed before saying goodbye to families because traveling exposes people to different challenges. The prayer, with the help of Allah, leaves a traveler at peace and eases him in his travels. Prophet Mohammad stated:

It is related that Ibn 'Abbas said, "The Prophet, may Allah bless him and grant him peace, once stayed somewhere for nineteen days during which he shortened the prayers. So when we travelled somewhere for nineteen days we would shorten the prayer but if we stayed longer we would do the full prayer."

It is related that 'Abdu'r-Rahman ibn Yazid was heard to say, "Uthman ibn 'Affan led us in prayer at Mina doing four rakats. 'Abdullah ibn Mas'ud was told about that and he said, 'We belong to Allah and return to Him!' Then he said, 'I prayed two rakats with the Messenger of Allah, may Allah bless him and grant him peace, at Mina and I prayed two rakats with Abu Bakr at Mina, and I prayed two rakats with 'Umar ibn al-Khattab at Mina. Would that I were lucky enough to have two out of the four rakats accepted!"

There is also a traveling supplication before exiting the house.

Traveling is highly emphasized in Islam for the Muslim community, because through traveling people not only learn knowledge in different sciences, but also open up to the world for business and propagating religion. As a matter of fact, Islam was spread by traveling merchants. The Qur'an states:

"Travel in the land and see what was the end of those who rejected truth." (Qur'an 6:11)[51]

By traveling, one can appreciate his life and what he has in life, thus, the Qur'an says: "And see those who reject faith, that is a clear indication of one's position intellectually, religiously, and socially in this world." For example, according to Islam, one has

---

[51] Qur'an 6:11

to be very clean and neat looking because that is a requirement of the faith. Thus, when he travels and sees someone that does not care for himself, even though there is enough water and accessibility of social hygiene, he appreciates his own faith more. According to Islam, it is by traveling that people become open-minded, discover and learn, because when people are exposed to different experiences and different things, it challenges their minds.

It is recommended that when a Muslim leaves his home, he should make a supplication; and when returning and entering his home, he should make a supplication. The following saying from the Prophet of Islam is as follows:

Entering the home

Bismillaahi walajnaa, wa bismillaahi kharajnaa, wa a'laa rab-binaa tawak-kalnaa.

In the name of Allah we enter, and in the name of Allah we leave, and upon our Lord we place our trust.

Leaving the home

Bismillaahi tawakkaltu 'a-lal-laahi walaa hawla walaa quwwata illaa billaah.

In the name of Allah, I place my trust in Allah, and there is no might nor power except with Allah[52].

Istikhara prayer

When a Muslim is in a state of doubt about his affairs, he performs the Istikhara prayer. Performed by two rakats of

---

[52] http://www.readwithtajweed.com/daily_duas.htm

prayers, desiring that Allah inspire him to do or not do what he plans to do. Inspired internally, he has complete submission to Allah and leaves all affairs to Allah.

Narrated by Jabir bin Abdullah: As-Salami: Allah's Apostle used to teach his companions to perform the prayer of Istikhara for each and every matter just as he used to teach the Surahs from the Qur'an. He used to say: "If anyone of you intends to do something, he should offer a two rakat prayer other than the compulsory prayers, and after finishing it, he should say: O Allah! I consult You, for You have all knowledge, and appeal to You to support me with Your Power and ask for Your Bounty, for You are able to do things while I am not, and You know while I do not; and You are the Knower of the Unseen. O Allah If You know It this matter (name your matter) is good for me both at present and in the future, (or in my religion), in this life and in the Hereafter, then fulfill it for me and make it easy for me, and then bestow Your Blessings on me in that matter. O Allah! If You know that this matter is not good for me in my religion, in my this life and in my coming Hereafter (or at present or in the future), then divert me from it and choose for me what is good wherever it may be, and make me be pleased with it." (See Hadith No. 391, Vol. 8) (Book 93, Hadith 487)[53]

53

http://www.searchtruth.com/searchHadith.php?keyword=Istikhara&translator=1&search=1&book=&start=0&records_display=20&search_word=all

ZAKA'T (CHARITY)

Zaka't is the third pillar of Islam, which makes a Muslim responsible for other fellow beings economically. Thus, Zaka't is the mandatory giving of a percentage of an individual's wealth towards charity. Zaka't is obligatory for every able bodied, sane Muslim. The economic principle of zaka't was established by Islam to eradicate poverty. The intent is bringing about a sustainable project for economic growth among the destitute, the poor, the orphans, and the widows with the hopes of giving an economic uplifting. In fact, in Islam, poverty would not exist if everyone paid their Zaka't. The word Zaka't means both purification and growth. Zaka't purifies the souls of those who give. For those Muslims who do not participate in paying Zaka't, on what Allah has blessed them with, there will be a great punishment on the Day of Judgment. However, it is important to note that Zaka't should only be paid by individuals who can afford to; as they will not sustain a hardship or forced to ask for the return of the money. Allah does not intend hardships for people. The obligatory nature of Zaka't can be found in several verses of the Qur'an and Hadith. It is related from Ibn 'Abbas, "The Prophet, may Allah bless him and grant him peace, sent Mu'adh to Yemen and said, 'Call on them to testify that there is no god but Allah and that I am the Messenger of Allah. If they comply with that, then let them know that Allah has made the five prayers obligatory on them every day and night. If they comply with that, then let them know that Allah has made the payment of Zaka't from their property obligatory on them, to be taken from the wealthy among them and given to the poor." (Bukhari 1331). Zaka't is mandatory for all men and women who are adults, working and those who possess property. Zaka't was decreed back from the time of Abraham. "We ,made them (Abraham and his sons) Imams who guided in accordance with our commandments, and we taught them how to work righteousness, and how to observe the Salat and the Zaka't. To us, they were devoted worshippers." (Qur'an 21:73)[54]. The Prophet Muhammad was the first who initiated the process of participating in Zaka't ,and his successor, Abu Bakr, was the first to initiate a statutory Zaka't system. Nowadays, in most Muslim countries, the system of paying Zaka't is voluntary and Muslims should give a portion of their wealth for their worship and love for God. In some countries, like Pakistan, Zaka't is obligatory and collected by the state. In other countries, like Jordan, where the system is regulated by the state, the amount an individual contributes is voluntary. Generally speaking, every adult male and female working, must pay 2.5 percent annually from their wealth; barring assets and certain personal use to the poor. However, the exact amount is not contained in the Qur'an, as Allah is all knowing and knows each individual's income, circumstance, and desire to do righteousness varies. Zaka't is mandatory when a certain amount of money, called the nisab, is reached or exceeded. If one owns less than the nisab, then Zaka't is not obligatory. Essential needs like food, clothing, shelter, transportation, and education, comprise the baseline of nisab; the minimum amount needed to sustain a family for a year at a reasonable level. If one's wealth passes the level of nisab, then the entire wealth is subject to Zaka't. Different schools of thought vary on when Zaka't is due, from monthly incomes, to once each lunar year. As an economic principle, the Sharia stipulated different percentages for gold and silver and other properties, including livestock, forcing one to go to the books of Zaka't and properly figure how much to pay annually. Zaka't is not only distributed for Muslims, but for needy non-Muslims as well; as Islam is a religion of humanity and not a group.

---

[54] Qur'an 21:73

Voluntary Alms (Sadaqa)

Where Zaka't is mandatory, there are other forms of charity that are also highly encouraged. Sadaqa, or voluntary alms, is one of such forms of charity that comes with great reward from Allah, but unlike Zaka't, because it is not mandatory. Sadaqa comes from the word truthful, and participating in Sadaqa exhibits ones true devotion to God. Sadaqa comes in many forms, including monetary, spreading love, giving good advice, or simply being a good person and not doing evil to others- all count as charity. When people give more alms to the needy, in the form of food, clothing, monetary, and any other way they can help, Allah will give them many rewards. The Qur'an states: "Men and women who have surrendered, believing men and women, obedient men and obedient women, truthful men and truthful women, enduring men and enduring women, humble men and humble women, men and women who give in charity, men who fast and women who fast, men and women who guard their private parts, men and women who remember God often, for them God has prepared forgiveness and a mighty reward." (Qur'an 33:35)[55] In giving alms, it is important that one not show off and be humble, not reminding people to whom he is giving alms; otherwise, his alms may not be accepted. Charity should be given in secret so as not to belittle those in need, or to embarrass, as is illustrated in many verses of the Qur'an, including: "If ye disclose acts of charity, even so it is well, but if ye conceal them, and make them reach those in need, that is best for you; it will remove from you some of your evil. And Allah is well acquainted with what ye do". (Qur'an 2:271)[56] Worship of Allah is not only found in praying and fasting. Any individual who strives to do good

---

[55] Qur'an 33:35
[56] Qur'an 2:271

deeds, and is constantly aware of the weak and poor, and aims to provide for their better welfare, is thought to be in a perpetual state of worship.   The Qur'an identifies the following eight groups of recipients of charity: "Verily the Sadawat (Zakah) are only for the poor and the needy and those employed to collect (the funds); and to attract the hearts of those who have been inclined (towards Islam); and to free the captives; and for those in debt; and for Allah's cause, and for the wayfarer; a duty imposed by Allah.   And Allah is All-Knower, All-Wise." (Qur'an 9:60)[57] When helping those in need, preference is given to those with a sense of dignity and respect for themselves. "A miskin (needy) is not the one who can be turned away with a date-fruit or two, or a morsel or two. The true Miskin is he who does not find enough to suffice him, does not disclose his poverty so that he might be given alms, and does not stand up to beg". (Bukhari) More so, the beggar who accumulates some wealth, the real needy, does not display need and poverty because of self respect, and thus, should be given aid first.

SAWM (FASTING)

Faith and Fasting

We have in our hands a Hadith of the Prophet Mohammed that states: "One thing that people do for God is fasting." Meaning, everything else Muslims do, such as prayers, charity, and zakat (mandatory poor due), is for their own sake. Despite the fact that fasting benefits people socially, morally,

---

[57] Qur'an 9:60

economically, politically and health wise (as the Prophet said, "fast to get healthy"), fasting is for the sake of God only.

WHY IS FASTING GooD FoR HEALTH?

The question then is why did Allah want His servants to be denied what is ordinarily legal, and have them suffer from hunger and thirst?

The relation between faith and fasting is very clear in verse 183 and 185 of chapter Al Baqarah (The Cow). We read: "O ye who believe! Fasting is prescribed to you as it was prescribed to those before you, that ye may learn self-restraint."(Verse 183). Verse 184 talks about the procedure of fasting, and Verse 185 Allah speaks to humanity about the importance of the month of Ramadan by saying: "Ramadan is the month in which was sent down the Qur'an, as a clear (sign) for guidance and judgment (between right and wrong)." There are several very important points contained within these two verses.

First, it is important to note that only people addressed for fasting are those that believe in Allah, because at the start of the verse Allah states: "O ye who believe!" Meaning, those who do not believe in Allah do not fast for Him, and also those who do not fast without lawful reasons are deficient in their beliefs.

Second, in these verses, it is commended that people should fast to "learn self-restraint." The only way for people to learn taqwa (piety) is through obedience to their Creator. Therefore, for a person to be able to distinguish the truth from falsehood, it is only possible through obedience to God, and in particular, through fasting. **I Do NoT BELIEVE THIS.**

Third, Allah speaks of His revelation of the Qur'an during the month of Ramadan. The Qur'an has also been called *Furquan*, meaning the book that distinguishes truth from falsehood. This is important in Qur'anology because in the Qur'an, words and verses are not placed beside one another by accident, rather there is the wisdom of Allah involved in each placement. Muslims fast for the sake of Allah during the month of Ramadan, in which the Qur'an was revealed. Because people cannot see Allah nor hear Him, they must then rely on the Qur'an for guidance and belief. What this tells us is that the Qur'an and fasting are both grounds for testing one's faith. Therefore, if one believes in Allah and the Qur'an, s/he will fast.

Allah has tested all of His Prophets and will test the *ummah* (Muslim community) as well. In Verse 155 of the above *Surah* (chapter), Allah says, "Be sure we shall test you with something of fear and hunger." Allah tests one's faith through fasting because fasting is a measure of truth and falsehood; and the measure of one's faith to his/her Creator, who is the Master of the Day of Judgment. It is important to note that fasting starts with *niah* (intention). Intention should be stated as such: *Wah bisamwa ghad nahwhyt min shar Ramadan* (I intend to fast tomorrow for the sake of Allah in the month of Ramadan). Also, before breaking the fast, the intention should be said like this: *Allahuma Ina Laka Sumtu wa beka amantu a alaika tawakultu wa Ala Riskeka Aftartu* (Oh Allah! I fasted for you, I believe in you, and I break my fast with your sustenance).

Socio-Psychological Principles of Fasting

Despite the fact that mankind, according to the Qur'an, is superior to all creatures, he is also a synthesis of good and bad qualities. Good emotions such as love, concern, compassion and kindness, and bad qualities such as envy, ill-thinking, filth of desire, jealousy and hatred all give a human being a sense of struggle within himself and toward society. Nurturing good qualities advances a human being towards God, while pandering bad qualities condemns a human being towards becoming a slave to his lusts. To control and suppress the dark side, one has to rely upon his Creator, the One who remembers His creatures at all times. God states in the Qur'an: "Those who forget God are made to forget themselves." (Qur'an 59:19)[58] One way to exalt the spirit of a human being is by fasting. It is with complete submission, constant remembrance of God, and through fasting that man may learn to control inherent evil desires. Fasting creates a challenging atmosphere for man because in a state of fasting, man is constantly in struggle to polish his inner soul and discipline his outer actions. Psychologically, fasting is a tool to control humans' mode of behaviors. By self-discipline, mankind controls thinking, attitude, and actions. God states in the Qur'an that fasting is prescribed so: "that you may learn self-restraint." (Qur'an 2:183)[59] By abstaining from food, drinks, and sexual desires, mankind overcomes lower desires and begins to realize his origin and to where he will depart from this life. When there is talk of complete submission to Almighty God during the month of Ramadan, Muslims are speaking of a total and complete fast from "tip to toe". Tip to toe means the mind fasts in order to keep the mind clear of ill-thinking. The eyes fast in order to not look at unlawful objects. The ears fast in order to not listen to offensive conversation, such as back-biting. The tongue fasts in order to not utter a word of gossip. Muslims' hands fast so that they do not perform unlawful actions. And Muslims' feet fast so that they do not venture towards places that displease God and distract their minds from His remembrance. It is because of this complete submission to God that the Prophet Mohammad stated: "God doesn't not accept the fasting of those who do not restrain from telling falsehood or from doing false deeds." It is this mode of behavior that endears an individual to society. And it is a person's actions and attitudes that are either accepted or rejected by others, and fasting shapes an individual's personality and relates him/her to society at large. This is why fasting has a

---

[58] Qur'an 59:19
[59] Qur'an 2:183

great impact on society, bonding people. Individual behavior is judged and justified according to one's actions towards society. Fasting upholds an individual's position in a social system. Fasting also promotes social equality among men and women. Rich and poor fast regardless of their social status, wealth, race, gender and so on. God only recognizes people on the basis of piety. There is also a degree of social responsibility that is equated with fasting. A Muslim who has the material means, but unable to fast due to health related reasons, must translate the duty of fasting into one of serving fellow humans by feeding a fasting indigent or non-Muslim poor person. Fasting is a socio-psychological phenomenon that purifies the soul and bonds men and women. It makes man more aware of his duty to submit to his Creator, by denying to himself what is ordinarily legal; it disciplines his/her sense of self-restraint, and positions him as a responsible social entity that recognizes social justice and equality. At the end of Ramadan, Muslims are required to pay Sadaqat ul-Fitr before the Eid festival. In the times of the Prophet, prior to the monetary system, people were encouraged to donate food, such as wheat and barley, to the less fortunate in order for everyone to have a meal on Eid. Nowadays, a form of payment to the less fortunate is acceptable. This charity is mandatory for all Muslims by the head of the household, and is between $5 to $10 dollars per family member in the household. For example, a family of three (father, mother, and one child), the sadaqat is $15 and has to be paid before the Eid festival. Another reason is if people make mistakes during the month of Ramadan while fasting, this charity washes out their minor wrongdoings by helping those who are less fortunate. Those who are single and live by themselves, and earn an income, are required to pay their own sadaqat.

Optional Fasting

As we have learned, fasting promotes purity of mind and heart, moving a person closer to his Creator. There are also optional fasts during the year that a person can commit to for his own spiritual fulfillment. Fasting on Monday and Thursday, according to one Hadith, will have a great reward from Allah; as accordingly the deeds of a person are registered on these two days. Next, fasting three days a month, on the thirteenth, fourteenth, and fifteenth of the lunar calendar. Third, fasting on the tenth of Muharram (Aushura). Fourth, fasting on the day of Arafah, in the month of Dhu Al-Hija. It should be noted that fasting on Arafah is not for those who perform Hajj. It is for those who are out of the Hajj ceremony; six days of Shawal (the month after Ramadan). Fasting on days, as desired, in the month of Shaban is also very rewarding.

HAJJ (PILGRIMAGE)

Hajj is the fifth pillar of Islam and mandatory once in one's lifetime; for adults who can afford it financially and possess good health. Hajj is an experience that Muslims gain not only for the Oneness of Allah, but the Oneness of the entire creation in which He created- Monotheism. Hajj shows that everyone, regardless of race, gender, language, and social status, are equal before Allah. There is no superiority but submission and piety in the way of Allah. It takes place the first ten days of the month of Dhu Al-Hija. Men are to wear a two piece white seamless cloth during Hajj, called Ihram. The significance of Ihram is that it makes all equal; symbolizes death; at the end of one's life, one will wear these two pieces of shroud, and stand before their Lord in the Hereafter. One symbolic meaning of Hajj is imitating the Hereafter while alive. It is a beautiful drama that Muslims play in this stage. The tawaf (circumambulation) of the Ka'aba seven times, symbolizes the seven heavens, where people start from the point where Prophet Abraham (Father of Monotheism) started, and end at the same point. This signifies that human beings all come from Him and return to Him. The seven runs between the heads of Safa and Marwa, called Sa'y, tell the believer to achieve his goals and objectives. People must work hard and struggle for what they want. Sa'y means struggle, to achieve a goal, and Muslims through Hajj are taught to work hard in this life; not only to reap the fruit of their hard work, but to reach Allah in the Hereafter. The proper Hajj begins on the eighth day of Dhu Al-Hija. All pilgrims go to Mina to meditate and worship overnight, per a tradition of the Prophet. The following day, they travel to Arafah, which is approximately nine miles from Mecca, for Wuquf (the standing). The place that people get together is called Jabal Rahma, "the mount of mercy". It is where the Prophet delivered his last speech. After Arafah, pilgrims go to Muzdalifa on the way back to Mina, where people spend the night. Hajj, in total, is evolution of mankind showing he is a part of the natural system and the natural system is a part of mankind. Circumambulating around the Ka'aba symbolizes orbit in the universe. Arafah, where people stay until sunset on the ninth day, is recognition of oneself and the existence of Allah. The word Arafah comes from Arf, which means to recognize. It was in this scene that Adam and Eve, when expelled from Heaven, recognized one another as human beings and understood the truth about their relation to God. Arafah teaches responsibility, not only towards God, but also towards humanity. People are required to pause at Mina. Literally, Mina means love, thus one attains mercy when pausing at Mina.

THE LAWFUL AND THE PROHIBITED IN ISLAM

One of the most important aspects of Islamic culture, from a cultural and anthropological point of view, is the rules of prohibition and what is permissible in Islamic life. Because Islam is a way of life, and mankind has been appointed as God's representative on Earth, it is then God who determines which foods are allowed for him to eat and what is not permissible to eat. Dr. Qaradawi clarified the issue in his book, "The Lawful and the Prohibited in Islam", stating: "The halal is that which Allah has made lawful in His Book and the haram is that which He has forbidden, and that concerning which He is silent He has permitted as a favor to you." Culturally, there are a number of points that one must pay attention to: one, the permissible and the prohibited are a clear guidance for conduct, health, and well-being. Two, it safeguards and protects people from evil minds. Third, the law of prohibited and permissible protects the environment from pollution and environmental disaster. Therefore, Islam does not allow harm to people, the environment, and society at large. What is important in the ruling of permissible and prohibited are things that are prohibited, the number is very few, while things that are permissible, the number is very vast. There are specific and explicit issues that have been prohibited by God; for example, eating pork, drinking alcoholic beverages, and gambling. And, from a socio-family point of view, adultery is prohibited. Another important issue regarding prohibited matters is what becomes permissible or prohibited according to the Prophet's actions and words. For example, the Prophet stated: "Whoever eats or drinks from gold or silver utensils is indeed filling his stomach with the fire of hell..." His Hadith is reported by Sahih Muslim. In another Hadith, reported by Al Bukhari, wearing silk garments and gold are prohibited as the Hadith states: "do not wear silk, for those who wear it in this life shall not wear it in the Hereafter." However, women wearing gold in a moderate fashion is permissible. The reason for this is if men wear silk and gold, it is a sign of superiority over other men and this superiority may indulge power and greed, which eventually leads to the abuse of others. According to the Qur'an, living a life of luxury leads to injustice, superiority of men over men, and discrimination of labor and those who are not well to do. History has shown that people of power and those who own the means of production, generally speaking, do exploit people for their own interests. The Qur'an says, "Thus when We intend to destroy a town for evildoing, We first command its affluent to become righteous."

This is important within Islamic Culture because it guides people with foods and also engulfs the entire being of a Muslim. The lawful and prohibited are the rights of God alone. No other may make things lawful or prohibited. According to Islam, Allah created human beings and He knows his needs, what he should eat, what to wear, how to behave, and in all matters is established either by the Qur'an or the traditions of the Prophet. Such prohibitions by God are laws. If one commits any of these acts, it is a major sin, and thus, in order to purify oneself from a major sin, one must repent and not repeat the sin. For example, adultery is considered a major sin. Before it is too late, one must repent. For minor sins, such as forgetting things unintentionally, being late to an appointment, or losing one's temper unnecessarily, the daily five times ritual prayers will wash away these sins. However, Muslims have two obligations. One, an obligation towards God, which he must guard His limits and not break His laws. Second is in dealing with people, starting with family members. These rights in Islam are called the Rights of God (haq ul Allah) and the Rights of Man (haq ul abd). To clarify these two, examples will be given. If one insults another, the Right of Man dictates that if the person insulted does not forgive, God will not forgive. On the other hand, the Right of God is His right and people are accountable in the Hereafter. For example, if a person does not pray intentionally, that is the Right of God to forgive or not to forgive. Prohibited (haram) and permissible (halal) constitute the entire modeling of Islamic culture, according to the men of knowledge in Islam. Those who commit wrongdoings and do not care about the permissible, while confessing to be a Muslim, are believed to be doing this out of ignorance and so are considered to be ignorant.

Prohibited and permissible cover all aspects of life. Therefore, it formulates and regulates Islamic culture socially, economically, politically and psychologically. Charging interest is considered exploitation of man by man in Islam, and thus, is prohibited. Nowadays, there are financial institutions, even in the United States, which function on an interest free banking system. Similar to the Jewish dietary formula of Kosher, Muslims have halal food that is permissible for consumption according to Islam. However, the decree of what is prohibited in Islam depends upon a person's situation, circumstance, and needs. The Islamic system is similar to a chain system, where every concept of life connects to another, and thus not separate. Therefore, all rulings and decrees function if the entire system is Islamic. Now, when people are living in the west, and the socioeconomic system is not Islamic, there are some exceptions. For example, interest rates are prohibited, but because Islam is not a way of life for deprivation and loss, interest rates are allowed in order for people to purchase a home or a car, as long as there is the intention to pay off the loan, and make the loan payment a priority in their life. This is due to not having any other choice or alternative in this western system. On the other hand, there are rules in Islam that are prohibited internationally, regardless of where one lives. For example, with bounties of food in markets, one does not need to eat pork's meat. However, if nothing can be found, no other form of sustenance is available, and the person is in a stage of starvation, then pork's meat is allowed to be consumed. Another example is alcoholic beverages, which are universally prohibited. However, if one is sick, and no other nonalcoholic medication is available, then he is allowed to drink syrup that contains a small amount of alcohol for his treatment.

PART FOUR

ISLAMIC CALENDAR AS A CULTURAL ENTITY

ISLAMIC CALENDAR

Islamic calendar has been established on the basis of a lunar cycle. The Qur'an talks about the lunar month as: "Splitter of morning light from the darkness- He alone made the night for repose and the sun and the moon for reckoning. That is that decree of the Overpowering One, the All-Knowing. And He alone is the One who made the stars for you, that you might be guided by them through the veils of darkness of land and sea. Truly, We have made the sign in creation utterly distinct indications for a people who would know God and His way." (Qur'an 6:96:97)[60]

The Islamic Calendar year began with the migration of Prophet Mohammed from Mecca to Yathrib. Yathrib was later called Medina by the Prophet. This migration took place July 16, 622 of the Christian Era. The lunar calendar consists of 12 months. The 12 months times 29.53 is equal to 354.36 days. Therefore, the Islamic lunar calendar is 11 days shorter than that of a solar year. The Islamic calendar has been utilized in all Muslim countries. However, Iran and Afghanistan converted the calendar to the Islamic solar calendar for administration purposes; yet, the Islamic lunar calendar is used for religious purposes. It is important to note that despite the fact that the lunar calendar can be calculated scientifically, Islamic Law requires two witnesses to observe the crescent moon personally and report it. This does not mean that Muslims do not believe in scientific principles. On the contrary, Muslims were pioneers of Astronomy and scientific principles. But to preserve the culture of Islam, it is a tradition (Sunnah of the Prophet Mohammed that two people should witness the crescent moon). Nowadays, for Muslims living all over the world, there are three kinds of

---

[60] Qur'an 6:96,97

crescent moon observations. One, Universal sighting, with the advent of new technology, scientists and astronomers are able to sight the moon with advanced instruments globally and report it. Only some countries accept this sort of moon sighting. Two, regional moon-sighting; for example in the United States and North America, to sight the moon regionally, and observe the new month. Third, local moon-sighting, is also a valid moon-sighting, especially in the month of Ramadan where the sunset and sunrise are different with a difference of 100 miles.

ISLAMIC MONTHS

1. Muharram, which means "forbidden" in Arabic. Muharram is the second most sacred Muslim month and includes the Day of Ashura.

2. Safar, which means "void".

3. Rabi-al-Awwal, which means "the first spring".

4. Rabi-al-Thani, which means "the second (or last) spring".

5. Jumada-al-Awwal, which means "the first month of parched land".

6. Jumada-al-Thani, which means "the second (or last) month of parched land".

7. Rajab, which means "respect" or "honor". Rajab is another of the sacred months in which fighting was traditionally forbidden.

8. Shaban, which means "scattered", marking the time of year when Arab tribes dispersed to find water.

9. Ramadan, which means "scorched". Ramadan is the most blessed month of the Hijri calendar, during which Muslims fast between sunrise and sunset. Also, the Qur'an was revealed in this month.

10. Shawwal, which means "raised", as she-camels used to get pregnant during this time of year.

11. Dhul-Qi'dah, which means "the one of truce". Dhu al-Qa'da was another sacred month during which war was banned.

12. Dhul Hijjah, which means "the one of pilgrimage", referring to the annual Muslim pilgrimage to Mecca, the Hajj. This is another of the four sacred months.

Unlike other calendar systems, the Islamic lunar calendar is not based on seasons in a year; it is shortened eleven days relative to the solar calendar. Therefore, each thirty-three year cycle, the pilgrimage (Hajj) and Ramadan (fasting) shall be observed in all seasons. Four out of the twelve months, Muharram the first month, Rajab the seventh month, Dhu Al Qa'da and Dhu Al Hija, the eleventh and twelve months, respectively, are called sacred months that are also called forbidden months. During these four months, battle has been prohibited. This has been emphasized by the Prophet in his farewell sermon, which was delivered on the 9th of Dhu Al Hijja. The reason these four months were determined as forbidden months date back to the pre-Islamic era, and Allah refers to it in the Qur'an as follows: "Indeed, the ordained number of the months with God is twelve lunar months, as was decreed in the

Preserved Heavenly Book of God on the day He created the heavens and the Earth. Four of them are sacred- and that is the upright religion- so do not wrong yourselves or others in them. Yet fight the warring idolaters, all together, even during them, just as all of them fight you therein. And know that God is with the God-fearing. As for the practice of deferring the observances of a sacred month, it is only an augmentation of the customs of unbelief by which those who disbelieve are led astray. They permit violating the sanctity of one year, and they prohibit it another year, to match the mere number of months that God has made sacred. Thus, they permit violating the sanctity of what God has made sacred, and the evil of their deeds is made fair-seeming to them therein. For God does not guide the disbelieving people."(Qur'an 9:36:37)[61]

IMPORTANT DATES IN THE ISLAMIC CALENDAR

- 1 Muharram (Islamic New Year)
- 10 Muharram (Day of Ashura)
- 12 Rabi al Awal (Mawlid an Nabi)
- 27 Rajab (Isra and Miraj)
- 15 Shaban (Mid-Shaban, or Night of Forgiveness)
- 1 Ramadan (first day of fasting)

---

[61] Qur'an 9:36,37

- 27 Ramadan (Nuzul Al-Qur'an)
- 1 Shawwal (Eid al-Fitr)
- 8-13 Dhu al-Hijjah (the Hajj to Mecca)
- 9 Dhu al-Hijjah (Day of Arafa)
- 10 Dhu al-Hijjah (Eid al-Adha)

Other Important Dates on Islamic Calendar

The birth date of the Prophet is on the 12th of Rabi al Awal. Many Muslims celebrate this day not only to commemorate the coming of the savior of humanity, but by seminars and conferences to remind themselves of the social, economic, political, moral, and ethical obligations that Mohammed brought to humanity. It should be noted, however, that the Shia school of thought celebrates the birth date of the Prophet on the seventeenth of Rabi al Awal.

Laylat Al Mir'aj, the Night of the Ascension, 27th of Rajab. This is the night that the Prophet ascended through the seven heavens on his night journey.

The Dome of the Rock which was built in 688-91 C.E. by the Umayyad Caliph Abdul Malik is an architectural masterpiece of the Islamic World in Jerusalem that commemorates the Night of Miraj. Miraj is the most important reason that Quds (Jerusalem) is a sacred place for Muslims. Peace in the region will not prevail unless Quds either returns to Muslims or is declared a neutral city for all faiths.

Laylat Al Bara'h- The Night of Forgiveness- 15th of Shaban. It is believed that in this night of Shaban, God Almighty will forgive his servants. On this night, people pray and recite the Qur'an and is very common among the subcontinent of India, Pakistan, Bangladesh, and Afghanistan.

ISLAMIC FESTIVALS/HOLIDAYS

Eid Ul Adha is the feast of the sacrifice on the 10th of Dhu Al Hijja, and it commemorates the sacrifice, obedience, and commitment of Prophet Abraham to Allah, who was ordered by Allah to sacrifice his son Ismail to Him. The significance of this festival, which also commemorates the last day of Hajj, is threefold. One, it shows the Islamic faith is not a separate religion but a continuation of the past Monotheistic faiths, namely, Christianity and Judaism. Therefore, it shows the continuity of history evolving based on the principle of Tawhid. Second, the drama and scenario of Hajj shows the universality of mankind within the universal system. The whole ritual shows unity of man as one single body and shows the bondage of man to God. It symbolizes the seven in the orbit when circling around Ka'aba seven times. Third, it tells the community that no one can reach Allah and attain felicity without trying (Sa'y) and sacrifice. In this sacrifice, a ram was given to Abraham by God and the tradition continues that every year Muslims, after completing their Hajj, sacrifice an animal such as a ram, goat, or a cow, for the sake of God. Again, the sacrifice is as much a religious ritual as also a symbolic ritual to teach mankind to perform any sacrifice for the sake of God in order to reach his own felicity. For example, if one person sacrifices his time for the sake of people or sacrifices his wealth for the sake of people, s/he has a lot of reward with God.

Eid Ul Fitr is the smaller festival in Islam which commemorates the end of the fasting month. This festival celebration by Muslims shows their sincerity to Almighty God because the purpose of fasting is to fast only for Him. It also is the celebration of their achievement that they fulfilled the command of Allah, their Creator. Third, the celebration of fasting is an acknowledgment of a Muslim that no one can reach God without going through some hardship.

The difference between the two festivals of Eid Ul Adha and Eid Ul Fitr is that on Eid Ul Fitr, on the first day when people are going for congregational prayer which is usually in the morning hours, they eat before they leave their homes. The common things between the two holidays is that people wear new clothes, join congregational prayers, and they visit each other's families and friends for expressing their joy of celebration by congratulating each other and saying, *"Eid Mubarak"* and enjoy tremendous amount of food, sweets and fruits (this occurs for three days for Eid Ul Adha). On these occasions, families wake up early in the morning and before going to prayers they set up their coffee tables with sweets, dates, cookies, and so on, making their home ready for receiving guests. It is not customary to call people and get appointments for their visit. Everybody goes to one another's house whether they are home or not. Traditionally, families go to their elders and then to the rest of their families and friends. The other difference between the other celebrations is that on Eid Ul Adha, after the five times daily prayers, a Muslim should recite *Takbirat* (La ilaha illalaa, There is no God but God). That starts on the day of Arafah and ends at the afternoon prayer (Asr) of the third day of Eid. This recitation occurs only on the day of Eid for Eid Ul Fitr.

27th of Ramadan, called Laylatul Al Qadr (Night of Power), is the night when angels descend for every issue of human life, bringing blessings of Almighty God to Earth. It is more valued than one thousand months according to the Qur'an. There is a chapter for this in the Qur'an that has five verses; the chapter is called Al Qadr, meaning: The Night of Empowering Decree. It is believed that on this night, the Qur'an was revealed. The chapter reads: "Indeed, it is We who have sent this Qur'an down from on high on the Night of Empowering Decree. And do you realize what is the Night of Empowering Decree? The Night of Empowering Decree is better than a thousand months! Therein do the angels and the Spirit Gabriel descend, by the permission of their Lord, with every divine commandment. Peace it is till the rise of dawn!" (Qur'an 97:1:2:3:4:5)[62] It should be mentioned that Muslims unanimously believe that the Night of

---

[62] Qur'an 97:1:2:3:4:5

Power was on the odd numbers of the last ten days of Ramadan, most likely the 21st and 27th of Ramadan. There is a specific prayer or supplication for the Night of Power. The beloved wife of the Prophet, A'isha, asked the Prophet what should she say if she happened to see Laylatul Al Qadr, and the Prophet replied to her stating: *"Allahuma innaka 'affuwwun tuhibbul 'afwa fa'fu 'anni'* (Oh Allah! You are the One who pardons greatly, and loves to pardon, so pardon me)."

Ashura, meaning the 10th, has important significances in the history of monotheism. On this day, the tenth of Muharram has three historical significances. One, the Prophet Noah left the Ark. Second, with the grace of God, Moses and the Jews were saved from the tyranny of Pharaoh in Egypt. Third, the grandson of Prophet Mohammed, Imam Hussein was martyred by the corrupt dynasty of Yazid. The commemoration of the martyrdom of Imam Hussein is held in respect every year by Muslims, both Shia and Sunni. However, the Shias take it more seriously because, according to the Shia school of thought, he was the third Imam of the Muslim community.

THE BLESSED DAYS OF ISLAM

It is believed the last ten nights of Ramadan are the best ten nights out of the year and the first ten days of the twelfth Islamic Month, Dhul Hijjah, are also the best ten days of the year as they encourage unprecedented acts of worship and Muslims throughout the world are encouraged to participate in various acts of worship. Amongst these actions, one of the best to partake in is for Muslims to perform Hajj. However, there are other ways to worship Allah during this time if a Muslim is not capable to perform the pilgrimage, including fasting the entire nine days, performing dikr, and takbeer. In fact, Muslims are encouraged to fast especially on the day of Arafah because the Prophet used to fast this day and said: "Fasting the Day of Arafah is expiation for (all the sins of) the previous year and expiation for (all the sins of) the coming year." (Bukhari, Muslim) Other ways of partaking in worship include repenting, reading the Qur'an, performing prayer all night, thanking Allah and performing good deeds.

PART FIVE

ANTHROPOLOGICAL ASPECTS OF FAMILY

EXTENDED FAMILY

There are two kinds of families in urban society, nucleus and extended families. Nucleus families are mostly established in western societies. The opinion of this author is that a nucleus family is derived out of individualism of western culture. A nucleus family consists of a husband, wife, and children. In this type of family, the husband and wife are responsible for their livelihood and their children's upbringing. Extended family is derived from a community oriented society. Islam is a religion of community; not of the individual. This doesn't mean individuals don't have rights or privileges, but their rights and privileges are tied to the welfare of the community, which is called the ummah. Anthropologically speaking, the concept of ummah is universal. In an Islamic sense, all Muslims are sisters and brothers. This principle bypasses all boundaries of gender, nationality, race, and language. A Muslim from Nigeria is a brother to a Muslim in America. This is the universality of Islam. Since an extended family is a derivative of the community, then the definition of immediate family is different than that of a nucleus family. In extended families, all uncles, aunts, grandparents, and cousins from both sides are all considered to be part of the family. Because they are a part of the family, they not only play a role in the upbringing of children, but they also have a right on each other as members of the family. For example, the brother of a father has almost the same right on a child as his father. By the same token, both sides play a major role in the upbringing of children for the construction of a cohesive bond for the family. Disrespecting one is disrespecting all.

WEDLOCK

Wedlock (Nikah) in Islam is a social contract not a sacred matrimony. It is a contract not based on civic laws but Qur'anic laws. It has been derived from the Qur'an and the tradition of the Prophet. Both parties have equal rights in proposing to one another. Both men and women can set forth conditions for their marriage. However, there is one condition on men that he has to offer a dowry to accept a woman. A dowry can take many forms, including a fund, property, or gift. Culturally, the reason for a dowry is that in case a divorce takes place, a woman should have enough assets to conduct a decent life and not resort to welfare or wrongdoing. The procedure is as follows: after proposal and acceptance, a very short verse from the Qur'an is recited and it follows: "O humankind! Be ever God-fearing, conscious of your Lord who created all of you from a single soul-and from it created its mate, and from them both spread abroad many men and women. So fear God, in whose name you ask consideration of one another. And, therefore, be dutiful to kindred. For, indeed ever is God vigilant over all of you." (Qur'an 4:1)[63] Some religious figures recite this verse before the proposal and acceptance and set the dowry amount. Some religious figures recite the above verse after the proposal and acceptance and set a dowry and witnessing of the witnesses. Both styles are acceptable. Witnesses are also a tradition of the

---

[63] Qur'an 4:1

Prophet to witness this contract. Witnesses should know the bride and groom well and they should witness that the two are mentally sound for marriage and that neither of them has any problem that would be an obstacle for their married life. Another responsibility of the witnesses is to be a witness in case there is a suspicion in the marriage. Nowadays, people record their marriage but, since it is a tradition of the Prophet during the marriage ceremony, it cannot be ruled out. In this distinguished gathering, some guests must be present and some food should be prepared. That is also a cultural norm within Islamic culture. In the beginning of Islam, people were marrying in the Mosque because the Mosque was the center of all Islamic actions. At the time of the Prophet, a marriage also took place at home. With changing times and development and economic prosperity of people, nowadays people prepare this ceremony in a banquet hall. It is all acceptable because a place of Nikah does not change the merit of Nikah. It is important to note that Muslims cannot marry infidels and polytheists (Mushrik). The Qur'an speaks about marriage in the following verses: "And He is the One who, from water, created a human being. Then He made for him kinship of blood and of marriage. And ever is your Lord all-able."(Qur'an 25:54)[64] Also: "And of His wondrous signs is that He has created for you, from yourselves, mates, so that you may repose in them. And He has set between you genuine mutual love and tenderhearted mercy. Indeed, in all of this there are sure signs for a people who would reflect on the handiwork of God." (Qur'an 30:21)[65] God speaks of the formation of the family as a sign of His blessing, stating: "Yet it is God alone who has made for you from among yourselves pairs, male and female. And He has made for you from your mates children and grandchildren. He has provided you, moreover, with all that is wholesome in

---

[64] Qur'an 25:54
[65] Qur'an 30:21

life. Then is it in falsehood they shall believe, while in the blessings of God they disbelieve?" (Qur'an 16:72)[66]

SEXUALITY IN ISLAM

For Muslims, based on an understanding of the Qur'an and Hadith, sexual relations are confined to marriage between a wife and husband. Within this context, the role of a healthy sexual relationship is extremely important. Having and raising children are encouraged among Muslims. Once a child is born, parents are expected to care for, nurture and prepare the child for adulthood, with a goal of imparting Islam so the individual is equipped with knowledge and willingness to accept and practice Islam and thus become a productive member of society.

The following is a discussion of sexuality in Islam provided by the Muslim's Women League:

In Islam, sexuality is considered part of our identity as human beings. In His creation of humankind, God distinguished us from other animals by giving us reason and will such that we can control behavior that, in other species, is governed solely by instinct. So, although sexual relations ultimately can result in the reproduction and survival of the human race, an instinctual concept, our capacity for self-control allows us to regulate this behavior. Also, the mere fact that human beings are the only creatures who engage in sexual relations once they are beyond the physical capacity for reproduction, sets us apart from all other species which engage in sex for the sole purpose of reproduction.

---

[66] Qur'an 16:72

Beyond childbearing, sexual relations assume a prominent role in the overall well-being of the marriage. In reading Hadith, one is impressed with the Prophet's ability to discuss all issues including those dealing with human sexuality. The topics range from questions about menstruation to orgasm. He apparently was not embarrassed by such inquiries, but strove to adequately guide and inform the Muslims who asked. Both the Qur'an and Hadith allude to the nature of sexual relations as a means of attaining mutual satisfaction, closeness and compassion between a wife and husband. "Permitted to you on the night of the Fasts is the approach to your wives. They are your garments and you are their garments."(Qur'an 2:187)[67] Also, Muslims are advised to avoid sexual intercourse during menses so as not to cause discomfort to the woman.

The goal of marriage is to create tenderness between two individuals and satisfy the very basic human need for companionship. "And among His signs is this, that He created for you mates from among yourselves, that you may dwell in tranquility with them, and He has put love and mercy between you; in this are signs for those who think."(Qur'an 30:21)[68] The Hadith which address this issue are numerous. The Prophet himself, while not divulging all aspects of his own sexual life, was known for his nature as a loving husband who was sensitive and physically demonstrative. In several Hadith, he speaks about the importance of foreplay and speaking in loving terms during sexual relations. Again, the concept of mutual satisfaction is elucidated in a Hadith which advises husbands to engage in acts that enable a woman to achieve orgasm first. Sexual dissatisfaction is considered legitimate grounds for divorce on the part of either wife or husband.

---

[67] Qur'an 2:187
[68] Qur'an 30:21

Sex Outside of Marriage

Naturally, attraction between individuals is necessary to initiate a relationship that leads to marriage. But sexual relations can obviously take place between any couple, consenting or not. Because of the far-reaching ramifications of sexual relations outside of marriage, Muslims are prohibited by God from such behavior. And because the process that leads to physical attraction and ultimately intimacy is part of human nature, Muslims are advised to behave in a way and avoid circumstances that could potentially result in extra- or pre-marital sex. Modesty in dress and behavior between women and men figures prominently as a means of exhibiting self-control. Similarly, unmarried couples are admonished against spending time alone in isolated places where they would be more likely to act on their feelings and thus be less inhibited.

Some of the negative results of sex outside of marriage include the potential for unwanted pregnancies, transmission of sexually transmitted diseases, disruption of the family and marriage (in cases of adultery), and emotional and psychological difficulties resulting from the lack of commitment associated with most relationships outside of marriage. As in other religions, extra- and pre-marital sex are considered major sins. Muslims believe that God does not simply forbid or allow behavior whimsically, but does so with our best interest at heart, guiding us away from potentially destructive behavior and towards behavior that allows us to achieve our most fulfilling potentials as human beings. For a similar reason, Muslims give up the consumption of alcohol because of faith in God's wisdom that the negative effects outweigh the positive for individuals and society at large. "Whoever submits his whole self to God, and is a doer of good, has grasped indeed the most trustworthy handhold..." (Qur'an 31:22)[69]

---

[69] Qur'an 31:22

Homosexuality

Human beings are capable of many forms of sexual expression, orientation and identification. The potential for behavior, such as homosexuality, does not mean that its practice is lawful in the eyes of God. Therefore, individuals are expected to control themselves and not act on their desires if such action is contrary to the guidelines of Islam. Homosexuality, like other forms of sexual relations outside of heterosexual marriage, is thus prohibited.

Any discussion of prohibited acts follows the question of what happens if they nevertheless occur. The Qur'an and Hadith are explicit regarding severe punishment by the State if a person is convicted of such a crime. However, in order for conviction to take place, the individuals must confess or be accused by at least four eyewitnesses of the act of actual intercourse. Obviously, the likelihood of these criteria being met is small which means that most couples who engage in unlawful acts will not be punished by the State. They will then deal with the consequences of their behavior in this life and will be accountable to God on the Day of Judgment. How He ultimately judges is known only to Him.

DRESS CODE

Dress, which technically means covering, has two aspects in Islamic Life. These two aspects are related to Muslim piety. Outer piety is the dress code that men and women wear and inner piety is the safe guarding of one's soul to keep the heart pure for the sake of Allah. That is why in Islam, as much as a dress code (Hijab) is important, at the same time, it is more important to safeguard one's intention and have a pure heart. The Qur'an alludes to both of these inner and outer pieties. As stated in the Qur'an, "O Children of Adam! We have, indeed, bestowed upon you a sense of want for clothing- to cover your private parts- and garments for adornment. Yet the garment of fearing God- that is the best of human adornment. This is of the manifest signs of One God, that they may remember His mercy and be thankful." (Qur'an 7:26)[70] Hijab is a dignified and modest way of dressing. Hijab is not a uniform. Nowhere in the Qur'an or in the Hadith of the Prophet Mohammed do we find a specification of a dress except what needs to be covered; both men and women are required to wear decent clothing. The Qur'an says, "Say also to the believing men, O Prophet, that they should lower their gaze from women that are forbidden to them and safeguard the chastity of their secret parts. That is most pure for them. Indeed, God is all-aware of all that they do. And say to the believing women, as well, that they should lower their gaze from men that are forbidden to them and safeguard their chastity of their secret parts, and not exhibit their own physical adornment, except what must necessarily appear thereof. Thus let them draw their veils over their bosoms and not exhibit their own physical adornment." (Qur'an 24:30:31)[71] Regarding the hijab, Professor Boisard writes, "There is nothing Islamic about wearing the veil which materially illustrates the inferiority of the Muslim woman. Mohammed recommended only that they behave in a modest fashion and that they cover their hair and necks with a scarf. It was apparently in Persia and the Near East that Islam encountered this custom in the cities. The Muslims adopted it for

---

[70] Qur'an 7:26
[71] Qur'an 24:30,31

psychological and social reasons, since in those days a woman who showed her face had the reputation of loose morals. This practice was maintained for a long time under the pressure of tradition, not through any religious obligation."[72]

GIFT EXCHANGE

Gift exchange is an Islamic tradition that promotes peace, harmony, friendship, and amicable relationship. In Islam, it is acceptable to receive gifts and be grateful. Wives can give gifts to husbands, husbands to wives, friends to friends, or strangers to strangers. In this tradition, a gift can be small or big; it does not matter. It is a matter of remembering someone. Also, when people feel close to each other, they can ask for a gift, even if it is something small like asking for a glass of water or milk. Of course, to the main importance of the Islamic tenet, a gift shouldn't be extravagant and people should take into consideration and practice moderation.

CHILD BIRTH

The coming of a child to a family is considered to be a blessing of God. This does not mean those who do not have a child are not blessed because God knows their goodness in life. Muslims sacrifice an animal (usually a lamb) when they are

---

[72] Boisard, *Humanism in Islam*

blessed with a baby to thank God for His gift. An elder person recites the Adhan in both ears of the child. The family decides to name him/her the most beautiful name they choose. Usually, for a male child, parents choose the names from the 99 attributes of Allah or Names of Allah. Naming girls is mostly after the well-known women figures of Islam, such as Fatima, the daughter of the Prophet, or literal names such as flowers, stars, and other adjectives. Also, many attributes of Allah can become a proper name for a girl by adding an "A" to make it feminine, such as Aziza, Hakima, or Halima.

ABORTION

Abortion is permitted in Islam under certain conditions. First, abortion is permissible for legitimate reasons and only within the first 120 days. After 120 days, abortion is prohibited. Within this time limit, abortion is permitted, if for any medical reason, the life of the mother is in danger, or for any medical reason, the child needs to be delivered earlier than the normal due date. Abul Fadl Mohsin Ebrahim, in his book *Abortion, Birth Control, and Surrogate Parenting: An Islamic Perspective Rights,* states: "Abortion may be sanctioned in the following three cases before the fourth month of pregnancy: if the doctors fear that the mother's life is in danger as a result of the pregnancy; if the pregnancy might cause a disease in the body of the mother; and if the new pregnancy severely reduces the mother's production of milk (lactation) and her already existing infant is absolutely dependent on its mother's milk for survival."[73] It is important to note that different schools of thoughts in Islam have different opinions about abortion. In the Hanafi School of Thought, which is the most flexible among the four, it is stated: " A valid reason for an abortion before the fourth month of pregnancy is required." The Maliki School states: "It is not permissible to induce the abortion once the semen has been retained in the womb even the first forty days of pregnancy." The Shafi' School considers abortion as a crime, stating: "The crime reaches maximum seriousness when it is committed after the fetus is separated alive."

WILL

Wills and testaments are an Islamic social principle to keep unity, respect, and peace among the community. The Qur'an states: "Prescribed for you believers, when death approaches any one of you who shall leave behind wealth, is that he make a will for his parents and nearest relatives, in accordance with what is right. This is an obligation upon the God-fearing. Thus whoever changes a will after hearing it from a testator, the guilt of sin shall fall only upon those who make the change in it. Indeed, God is all-hearing, all-knowing. Yet as to one who fears erroneous inclination from the testator, or willful violation of the heir's due right and who then sets matters aright

---

[73] Abul Fadl Mohsin Ebrahim, *Abortion, Birth Control, and Surrogate Parenting: An Islamic Perspective Rights*

between them, no guilt of sin shall fall upon him. Indeed, God is all-forgiving, mercy-giving."(Qur'an 2:180, 181, 182)[74] In an Islamic will, one can distribute his wealth and advise people what needs to be done. According to the book of Wills and Testaments of Sahih Bukhari Volume 4 Hadith 3 and 4 the Prophet did not leave any wealth behind to be distributed nor did he appoint anyone to be appointed as the leader of Muslims. According to Sunni Islam, Hadith number 4 states: "Narrated Al-Aswad: In the presence of Aisha some people mentioned that the Prophet had appointed Ali by will as his successor. Aisha said, "When did he appoint him by will? Verily when he died he was resting against my chest (or said in my lap) and he asked for a wash basin and then collapsed while in that state and I could not perceive that he had died, so when did he appoint him by will?"[75] According to this Hadith, Sunni Islam rejects the appointment of Ali as successor of Mohammed. This is not the view of the Shia Ulema on this matter. In Islamic law, whatever the deceased leaves behind is distributed among his heirs according to a certain ratio. People are allowed also to give one third of their property to others than their legal heirs. Islam not only recommends a will to be written but strongly emphasizes that people should give their wealth and property as charity to the poor and destitute and those who are in need.

DIVORCE

Divorce is permitted in Islam but it is highly recommended to avoid, if possible. It is the last resort when there is no other alternative for a couple. A couple has been advised to

---

[74] Qur'an2:180, 181, 182
[75] Sahih Bukhari Volume 4 Hadith 3 and 4

work out their differences and stay together. The Qur'an says, "Pronouncement of divorce is revocable two times. Each time thereafter, wives are to be retained, in accordance with what is right, or set free with generous kindness. Moreover, it is not lawful for you to take back anything in divorce of what you have given them-unless both have cause to fear that they will not be able to maintain the ordained limits of God in their settlement. So, if you who judge between them have cause to fear that they will not be able to maintain the ordained limits of God, then there shall be no blame on either of them in that which she may compensate the husband, for her parting. Thus these are the ordained limits of God, so do not transgress them. For whoever transgresses the ordained limits of God, then it is such as these who are the wrongdoers, accountable before Him." (Qur'an 2:229)[76] From the above verse we also understand that a man and a woman can get back together and reconcile if the word of divorce is uttered twice. So Islam gives an opportunity to people to think over about their relationship instead of making a sudden one time decision. After the third utterance of divorce it is final. There is a misunderstanding among Muslims and non-Muslims that a woman cannot seek divorce. The matter of fact is that the woman can seek divorce and the man should fulfill that request and if he does not then the court of law should divorce the woman. The issue of divorce is so important in Islam that an entire chapter called Divorce (Talaaq), which is chapter 65 of the Qur'an, is allocated for this purpose and all the rules and regulations and conditions of divorce have been illustrated in that chapter. There are some principles of divorce according to the Qur'an and the tradition of the Prophet Mohammed. The Qur'an says, "O Prophet! When you who believe intend to divorce women, then it shall not be during menstruation- nor shall you have intimate relations with them thereafter- rather

---

[76] Qur'an 2:229

divorce them at the beginning of their prescribed waiting period, and count the exact days of the prescribed waiting period- and fear God, your Lord. (Qur'an 65:1)[77] So the first principle of divorce, according to the Qur'an, is that women should not be divorced during their menses and they need to be "clean". The second principle of divorce is there should be two witnesses. The Qur'an says, "Moreover, let two just men from among you bear witness to this outcome. And you who are witnesses shall administer upright testimony, for the sake of God." (Qur'an 65:2)[78] The third principle of divorce is if one is not sure and is uncertain about a woman's term their waiting period shall be three months. The Qur'an says, "As to those of your women who anticipate no further menstruation- if you are uncertain as to their term- then their waiting period shall be three months, just as it shall be for those who have not yet menstruated."(Qur'an 65:3)[79] The fourth principle is that pregnant women are not supposed to be divorced until their delivery. As the Qur'an says, "As for those who are pregnant, their stated term is whenever they deliver what they carry." (Qur'an 65:4)[80] The fifth principle is that no one can get a woman out of her home until their period is over. They should not be harassed and should not leave without sustenance. The Qur'an says, "So as to the wives you proceed to divorce, give them residence throughout their waiting period in the homes where you reside- in accordance with your means. Yet you shall not harass them, so as to cause them distress. (Qur'an 65:5)[81] It is important to note that different schools of thought have different rulings for divorce. For details and information on the issue of divorce, one has to resort to different schools of thought as needed. There are four conditions of divorce. One,

---

[77] Qur'an 65:1
[78] Qur'an 65:2
[79] Qur'an 65:3
[80] Qur'an 65:4
[81] Qur'an 65:5

either party must be in a sound state of mind. Two, there should not be any external pressure that means that no one can force anyone to divorce. Three, the intention should be clear and for the purpose of good will of both parties. Fourth, the wife must be in the state of purity.

As we know, culture in Islam is not static and it is a moving dynamic and change-oriented phenomenon. Problems occur within marriages in the following instances: one, the Islamic culture becomes heavily influenced by indigenous non-Muslim cultures. In some instances, indigenous culture justifies their culture based upon Islamic values. For example, female circumcision is not an Islamic tradition but people in some African countries use a weak Hadith justifying their action. Two, the dogmatic approach of interpretation (tafseer) of the Qur'an has distorted the true nature of Islamic culture. A good example of that is the approach of some ulemah to the Qur'an and the Sunnah of the Prophet. Their dogmatic interpretation caused thousands of deaths, animosity, and criminal acts around the world. The attack of 9/11 is a direct result of interpretation of the Qur'an by some ulemah. Three, in a contemporary world, a majority of Muslims remain illiterate. Illiteracy is more common among women who are supposed to be the first educators of the family. This mass illiteracy is against Islamic culture and caused by misapplication of Islamic law. A good example is the stoning to death of unjustified adulterers by the Taliban.

PART SIX

ISLAMIC DIETARY LAW

FOOD AND DIET

Anthropologically speaking, food and diet in Islam is an important and vital principle because it is through proper meal and diet that one gains energy and is ready to perform duties. Most importantly the purpose of eating in Islam is not just to satisfy biological needs but to gain energy to worship God. God says in the Qur'an, "O you who believe! Eat of the wholesome foods which We have provided for you. And give thanks to God, if, indeed, it is He alone whom you worship."(Qur'an 2:172)[82] There are some principles of food in Islamic law. The first principle is that Allah knows His creation. He knows what his creation should eat and what not to eat. Understanding the human system, Allah determined what humankind can consume because human beings are both carnivorous and omnivorous that means that they eat both meat as well as vegetables. The Qur'an says, "Indeed, He has but forbidden you to eat carrion, and blood, and the flesh of swine, and that over which other than the name of God has been invoked at the time of slaughter." (Qur'an 2:173)[83] "And recall when you said, thereafter: O Moses! Never shall we endure with patience one kind of food. So call upon your Lord for us, to bring forth for us some variation from what the Earth grows- of its herbs and its cucumbers, and its garlics, and its lentils, and its onions." (Qur'an 2:61)[84] From the above verses, we understand that certain meats, including swine meat, is forbidden in Islamic diet. The second principle is that food should come from a rightful source. That means that if one earned income from prohibited sources, then it is also forbidden in Islam. A good example is partaking in gambling, stealing, and fraudulent actions to make money. The reason for this is that Islam wants a community where members should conduct a

---

[82] Qur'an 2:172
[83] Qur'an 2:173
[84] Qur'an 2:61

decent life and earn with honesty and integrity. Consequently, they should live in peace by themselves. The third principle is that it has been recommended that people should eat with moderation and eat as little as possible and avoid overeating. The fourth principle is that, according to the law of Islamic diet, a meal should be eaten slowly and chewed properly. Fifth, it is not allowed to express dislike for any food. If someone does not like a food instead of showing his hatred towards that food he should politely refuse taking it. Sixth, people should know their nature and eat according to what their nature requires. Sometimes some fruit or vegetable may not suit a person and it might suit someone else. This is not because that fruit or vegetable is bad, it is because it just does not fit their nature. Seventh, each meal or drink should be consumed with the name of Allah saying, "I begin in the name of Allah most Gracious, most Merciful." At the end of the meal people should offer thanks to Allah by saying, "Oh my lord! Thank you for the food, for the water and that you made me a Muslim". Eighth, people should wash their mouth after consuming meals. Ninth, there is also another supplication by the Prophet that says, "Praise to be to Allah. Much and good praise. Oh our Lord, we cannot compensate your favor nor leave it nor dispense with it." (Bukhari)[85] On the authority of Abu Hurayrah, the Messenger of Allah said: "Your body has a right on you", and "Be keen to do what is of benefit to you."

Health: Allah's Blessing - Natural Food

As we said earlier, Tawhid is universal and it aligns with all aspects of creation. Below is proof of the universality of Tawhid regarding food and the body system. Allah left us a great clue as to which foods help certain parts of our body in what has been coined the "Doctrine of Signatures" by the Swiss physician Paracelsus who strongly believed that man and the universe are the same. This concept states that the physical form of a food

---

[85] Hadith number 368, The Book of Food, Sahih Al Bukhari Volume 7

help give a clue as to its healing purposes. A sliced carrot looks like the human eye. The pupil, iris and radiating lines look just like the human eye and science now shows carrots greatly enhance blood flow to and function of the eyes. A tomato has four chambers and is red. The heart has four chambers and is red. All of the research shows tomatoes are loaded with lycopine and are indeed pure heart and blood food. Grapes hang in a cluster that has the shape of the heart. Each grape looks like a blood cell and all of the research today shows grapes are also profound heart and blood vitalizing food. A walnut looks like a little brain, a left and right hemisphere, upper cerebellums and lower cerebellums. Even the wrinkles or folds on the nut are just like the neo-cortex. We now know walnuts help develop more than three (3) dozen neuron-transmitters for brain function. Kidney beans actually heal and help maintain kidney function and yes, they look exactly like the human kidneys. Celery, rhubarb and many more look just like bones. These foods specifically target bone strength. Bones are 23% sodium and these foods are 23% sodium. If you don't have enough sodium in your diet, the body pulls it from the bones, thus making them weak. These foods replenish the skeletal needs of the body. Avocadoes, eggplants, and pears target the health and function of the womb and cervix of the female - they look just like these organs. Today's research shows that when a woman eats one avocado a week, it balances hormones, sheds unwanted birth weight, and prevents cervical cancers. And how profound is this? It takes exactly nine (9) months to grow an avocado from blossom to ripened fruit. There are over 14,000 photolytic chemical constituents of nutrition in each one of these foods (modern science has only studied and named about 141 of them). Figs are full of seeds and hang in twos when they grow. Figs increase the mobility of male sperm and increase the numbers of sperm as well to overcome male sterility. Sweet potatoes look like the pancreas and actually balance the glycemic index of diabetics. Olives assist the health and function of the ovaries. Oranges, grapefruits, and other citrus fruits look just like the mammary glands of the female and actually assist the health of the breasts and the movement of lymph in and out of the breasts. Onions look like the body's cells. Today's research shows onions help clear waste materials from all of the body's cells. They even produce tears which wash the epithelial layers of the eyes. A working companion, garlic, also helps eliminate waste materials and dangerous free radicals from the body. A physically able believer is better than a weak believer.

Whereas running to the pharmacy for an ailment to cure a sickness is very common in western societies, many Islamic countries turn to natural remedies. Food can be used as the best medicine to combat many major illnesses, including heart disease, cancer, allergies, and diabetes. For instance, green tea is great for the immune system and can suppress one's appetite. Food like local honey and yogurt can help combat symptoms of allergies. Honey can also serve as a sedative if one has problems with insomnia. People with bone problems can consume pineapples to help fight off osteoporosis because pineapples contain manganese and boost immunity. Fish contains omega oils which can help combat arthritis. Women who are pregnant should consume ginger to help cure nausea and women suffering from bladder infections should drink cranberry juice which help contain the growth of bacteria. For asthma, one should eat onions because onions help ease the constriction of the bronchial tubes. If one has an upset stomach, bananas should be consumed because bananas will settle an upset stomach. If one has memory problems, they should eat oysters because oysters help improve mental functioning by supplying zinc. Consumption of garlic can help lower cholesterol levels, as well as consumption of avocados. Blood pressure can be lowered too by eating celery and olive oil. Those who suffer from breast cancer should eat wheat, bran, and cabbage as these food items help to maintain healthy levels of estrogen. A good antidote for lung cancer is to eat dark green and orange vegetables because these contain beta carotene, a form of Vitamin A. Those suffering from ulcers should eat cabbage as cabbage contains chemicals that help heal certain types of ulcers, and those suffering from diabetes should eat broccoli and peanuts as the chromium in these two food items helps regulate insulin and blood sugar.

DIET AND FAITH

Many people are unaware of connections between diet and religion and they seek various man made theories of nutrition and diet, some of which are in contradiction to the human physiological being. According to Islam, God created mankind and He knows precisely what man needs for his proper growth and development. It is an important facet in life to realize and recognize the role of God in every walk of life. With His comprehensive knowledge, He has ordained the consumption of certain types of foods, and has prohibited others.

In addition, psychologists have studied the effect of what humans eat and its effect on the brain and its function. It is largely believed that pig meat affects the chemistry of the brain. As the saying goes, "you are what you eat". For example, it is commonly evident that vegetarians are mild in character and behavior. Also, consumption of alcohol is known to affect the mood and personality of a person, and is well documented to be at the root of the many evils in today's society, aside from its physiological damage to the individual.

Among the three monotheistic religions, namely Judaism, Christianity, Islam, it is the religion of Islam that envelopes its teachings within it a comprehensive prescription for diet. The reason for this is that according to Islam, having a proper diet and proper eating habits are a part of worshiping God. The Qur'an declares that God created the Jinn and mankind simply to worship Him. This worship is not only a set of rituals, but it encompasses actions and all aspects of life. For example, in the present context, following dietary habits in conformance with the laws of God is a form of worship. In the larger context, worship and its other forms can likewise not be adequately performed or accepted without the use of permissible sources of energy. Prophet Mohammed once mentioned that a person lost in a desert turns his face to the sky and implores his Lord for help but how can he expect his prayers to be answered when his food and clothing are illegally derived. Therefore, not only is it important that we should consume food, but also, it should be obtained by honest and legal means. This is because humans are comprised of body and soul, and diet should harmoniously complement both these aspects of an individual so that a person can grow both physically and spiritually.

There are five major sorts of injunctions related to diet. First, as mentioned above, its consumption must be permissible by God. According to the Qur'an, God created different types of foods to sustain his different creatures. In Surah Hud 11:6, He says, "there is no moving creature but its sustenance depends on God; he knows the time and place of its definitive abode and its temporary deposit all is in a clear record." What this verse tells us is that if we consume something that is not permissible we have strayed from a norm of our creation and therefore, are susceptible to harm. A good example, again, is regarding the consumption of alcohol.

The second is cleanliness. The Qur'an says that God loves those who are clean. This cleanliness applies not only to eating habits, but also to the total aspect of the individual and the environment. A person has to wash their hands and mouth, both before and after the meal according to the tradition of the Prophet Mohammed. Social hygiene is a prime importance and if the food is clean, if the environment is not, this can pose a health hazard. A Muslim scientist named Al-Razi (Razhes in Latin) was the first to prescribe alcohol as an antiseptic in the tenth century. Indeed, the word alcohol is derived from the Arabic language.

The third is that the diet must suit a person's nature according to Islam. Everyone has his own nature. Since natural entities need to know their nature before consuming any food item. For example, there are many children who are allergic to peanuts. That does not mean that peanuts are unlawful to eat but it does not suit some children's health. For example, a husband may really like chili but a wife may not be able to handle the spicy food. It does not mean that it is bad, it just means that the two have different natures. This is applicable to all aspects.

The fourth injunction is that food has its own nature just like human beings. Human beings are natural entities so are food natural entities. Both have their nature. According to Islamic dietary system, food is categorized as cold and warm. And that has direct effect to human bodies. For example, ginger is considered to be warm food. And when people consume ginger, they feel warm. By the same token, cucumbers are considered to be cold food. Usually, in the Middle East, cucumbers are consumed during hot summer days because it cools down the system. Another example are walnuts, which are considered to be warm food. And those who have cold natures when consuming walnuts feel warmer. Having said this, it is important, according to Islamic dietary system, that people should know their nature and consume what is good for them. Otherwise, they may have either bad reactions or feel sick.

The fifth injunction is meat. All meat are not good for human nature. For example, pork is prohibited because for a variety of scientific reasons, it is harmful to the body. In Judaism, as well as in Islam, consumption of pork meat or derivatives is forbidden. It has been scientifically established that pigs don't have sweat glands and hence, they do not secrete toxins as well as other animals do. As a result, their meat is readily spoiled and prone to carry various disease-causing pathogens.

PART SEVEN
ISLAMIC FINE ARTS

What is interesting in Islamic art and architecture is that everything corresponds to the philosophy of Tawhid, which is oneness of God with the universe. In art and architecture, everything not only corresponds with each other, relates to each other, but also brings peace and harmony to the soul. Again, this peace and harmony of art and architecture symbolically presents the meaning of Islam, which is peace. Another aspect of art and architecture in Islam is that they are interwoven. A building by its own nature should be a piece of art. Art by its own nature should be a universal concept. This means that art and architecture is a symbol of unity of man with God. For this reason, Muslim artists from the very beginning shun away from those concepts of art that do not represent unity. The best way to formulate unity is to use mathematics and geometry. Geometrical designs symbolize a universal system with its stars or patterns of designs within our natural system. Learning from the universal system and the design patterns of natural law gave Muslim architects the idea to introduce a nine-sided polygon, the nonagon, within architectural designs. The representation of art and architecture in Islam is a manifestation of God. For example, "With the navel as the centre of the circle, which represented the Earth, and the place of life sustenance, this demonstrated a divine manifestation. These divine proportions were reflected in cosmology, musicology and calligraphy, and in all arts from the 10th century." Another example of this manifestation is the domes of the buildings that symbolize the universe or fountain and gardens that represent paradise. As the Qur'an says, "Surely the God fearing shall be among gardens and fountains." (Qur'an 51:15)[86]

---

[86] Qur'an 51:15

QUR'AN AND SCIENCE

The philosophy of Tawhid as we learned throughout this research dictates not only oneness of God but oneness in relation to His creation. In Islam everything must be derived from Tawhid. All aspects of life must be studied and analyzed based on Tawhid. That means anything in life not related to Tawhid is not Islamic. Science and culture is an issue that Islam puts a great emphasis on. Since God is knowledge and pure knowledge, culture and science cannot be separated from Tawhid. Ms. Carly Fiorina, Chief Executive Officer of Hewlett-Packard Corporation, said the following on the importance of science and culture in Islam:

"There was once a civilization that was the greatest in the world. It was able to create a continental super-state that stretched from ocean to ocean from northern climates to tropics and deserts. Within its dominion lived hundreds of millions of people, of different creeds and ethnic origins. One of its languages became the universal language of much of the world, the bridge between the peoples of a hundred lands. Its armies were made up of people of many nationalities, and its military protection allowed a degree of peace and prosperity that had never been known. The reach of this civilization's commerce extended from Latin America to China, and everywhere in between. And this civilization was driven more than anything, by invention. Its architects designed buildings that defied gravity. Its mathematicians created the algebra and algorithms that would enable the building of computers, and the creation of encryption. Its doctors examined the human body, and found new cures for diseases. Its astronomers looked into the heavens, named the stars, and paved the way for space travel and exploration. Its writers created thousands of stories. Stories of courage, romance and magic. Its poets wrote of love, when others before them were too steeped in fear to think of such things. When other nations were afraid of ideas, this civilization thrived on them, and kept them alive. When censors threatened to wipe out knowledge from past civilizations, this civilization kept the knowledge alive, and passed it on to others. While modern Western civilization shares many of these traits, the civilization I'm talking about was the Islamic world from the year 800 to 1600, which included the Ottoman Empire and the courts of Baghdad, Damascus, and Cairo, and enlightened rulers like Sulayman the Magnificent. Although we are often unaware of our indebtedness to this other civilization, its gifts are very much a part of our heritage. The technology industry would not exist without the contributions of Arab Mathematicians."

The reason that science and knowledge is the foundation of Islamic culture is because mankind cannot understand and comprehend his own existence without grasping knowledge. That is why the Prophet of Islam said, "The one who knows himself knows God." Therefore, science is an integral part of Islamic culture and a Muslim without science and understanding of the world cannot normally conduct a functional life. One reason that a percentage of Muslims are backward today is because they left their responsibility towards science to the contemporary world. In the following verses of the Qur'an, the contributions of Muslims to world civilizations are mentioned: "We have honored the children of Adam." (Qur'an 17:70)[87] The dignity and integrity of mankind is through knowledge after piety. In the Qur'anic verse, "O my Lord! Advance me in knowledge." (Qur'an 20:14)[88] And the positions that men of

---

[87] Qur'an 17:70
[88] Qur'an 20:14

knowledge were highly emphasized in the Qur'an opened academic principles, universities, and halls of wisdom. Those verses are as follows: "Only scholars will be able to reason it out." (Qur'an 29:43)[89] Say: "Those who know and those who don't, will they ever be equal." (Qur'an 39:9)[90] "Allah grants wisdom to whom He pleases; and whoever is so granted has been given good indeed. For only those with sharp minds will be able to grasp." (Qur'an 2:269)[91] It was this emphasis of Qur'an that Baitul Hikma (house of wisdom) opened in Baghdad, Al Ahzar University opened in Egypt, and Al Qarawiyin was built in Morocco. Another reason that religion and science and science and culture in Islam are tied together is because the Arabic word for university is Jami'ah and the feminine form of the Arabic word is Jami. Hence, knowledge taught in the mosques and universities is an offshoot of mosque learning and educating masses. So in Islam, Jami (mosque) has not been a place of just praying to Almighty God, but rather it was an environment for worshipping God through pure knowledge. This definition of learning through the mosque where God Almighty is being worshipped can clearly be seen in the following verse: "He who taught (the use of) the pen and taught man that which he knew not." (Qur'an 96:4 & 5)[92] The legacy of Islamic science and knowledge to the world is not only the contribution Muslims made to the world of civilization, but also a tradition that remained with us until now. The tradition of graduations of universities today come from Muslim universities, such as the gown that is worn at graduation. The word chairman at the universities also came from Muslim centers of learning where the Master either sat on a chair or the Minbar of the Mosque, and

---

[89] Qur'an 29:43
[90] Qur'an 39:9
[91] Qur'an 2:269
[92] Qur'an 96:4 and 5

students sat on the floor in front of him. The tassel on the graduation cap comes from Al Ahzar University of Egypt, which was founded in 972, and is still standing as a prominent Muslim center of learning in the world. Three Hadiths of the Prophet of Islam make Muslims responsible to gain knowledge. Those are as follows: "Learning is mandatory for all men and women." Second, "Seek knowledge even in China"; and third, "If anyone travels on a road in search of knowledge, Allah will cause him to travel on one of the roads of Paradise." Muslims made an enormous contribution in the field of science and technology and for the record we would like to name a few. Al- Idrisi who was a European Muslim showed that the Earth was spherical. Ibn Battuta travelled for 29 years through different lands and recorded lifestyle, trade, historical places, and he is considered to be a travel reporter of his time. His book opened the doors for understanding other cultures, norms and values, geography and climate. Al- Khwarizimi is the founder of algebra. Al-Biruni laid the foundation of trigonometry. Jabir ibn Hayyan is the founder of chemistry and the word chemistry comes from the Arabic root kimyaa. Al-Razi is another Muslim scientist who created distilled perfumes. These were a few Muslim men of knowledge.

The Qur'an was revealed fourteen centuries ago in the seventh century and within its text, includes miracles that serve as another testament to God's existence and His word as a source of true knowledge. Scientific revelations are described in the Qur'an centuries before the scientific community made these discoveries. Allah's word is further validated as modern-day technology and knowledge prove scientific facts which are described in the Qur'an years before such technology was available. There is no way that mankind had the knowledge or resources in the seventh century to discover the scientific revelations mentioned in the Qur'an, which again proves Allah is the Lord of the Universe and All-Knower of everything.

CALLIGRAPHY

Calligraphy emerged as an art form because Islam rejected the idea of human figures in places of worship. However, Muslims developed miniature art that used the human figures mostly depicting royal courts, bathrooms, wars, agriculture, and so forth. That means, using human figures as art is permissible but not as an object of worship. With the use of geometry, Muslim artists created and developed a new art form called Arabesque. B. Dobree, an art historian, said, "Arabesque strives not to concentrate the attention upon any definite object, to liven and quicken the appreciative faculties, but to diffuse them. It is centrifugal, and leads to a kind of abstraction, a kind of self-hypnotism even, so that the devotee kneeling towards Mecca can bemuse himself in the maze of regular patterning that confronts him, and free his mind from all connection with bodily and Earthly things." Arabesque is not only in the form of script but floral and geometric patterns. The whole idea of Arabesque and the Islamic art is not only to create art but to show that the universe is one unit connected with each other. Beautifying the Mosques with calligraphy of the verses of the Qur'an relate people to God. Through seeing, reading, and thinking, a person would see himself as an entity not detached from the universal system. According to the Qur'an, God taught mankind the use of the pen and therefore, the pen became a symbol of knowledge and contributed to the art of calligraphy. Calligraphy has a strong cultural connotation within Islamic culture that gives a personality and a vision to those who perform it. That means those who write beautifully are in love with knowledge. In another word, calligraphy depicts the goodness of heart in an individual. He is attentive, concentrating and detail oriented so he indulges himself thoroughly into the universal system through calligraphy.

MAGIC AND FORTUNE TELLING

Islam is established on the basis of knowledge and through worshipping Allah. It rejects any form of fortune telling and magical work because these works are not knowledge-based. It is considered to be an evil work. The Qur'an asks people to seek refuge from those who perform these evil works, saying: "And from the evil of sorceresses who blow upon knots to cast spells."(Qur'an 113:4)[93] Culturally, Islam commanded people to stay away from suspicion because suspicion is not knowledge-based and a good Muslim should rely on truth theologically and scientifically. As the Qur'an states, "O you who believe! Shun much suspicion. For, indeed, certain kinds of suspicion are sinful."(Qur'an 49:12)[94] In another verse, Allah states: "Though they have no sure knowledge therein. They follow nothing but mere conjecture- and conjecture avails nothing at all against the truth."(Qur'an 53:28)[95]

STORY TELLING

Story telling has a strong cultural significance in the cultural anthropology of Islam. The Qur'an reveals past stories that happened with the past people as a sign of maxim, learning, and warning for future generations. Narrations of the Qur'an reveal the truth about the mistakes of the past generation as a warning that the Muslim community should not make the same mistakes. It is through the stories of the Prophets and the people

---

[93] Qur'an 113:4
[94] Qur'an 49:12
[95] Qur'an 53:28

that the Qur'an put a significant emphasis on history. Through understanding history, people can make sound decisions. According to the Qur'an, it is through the stories and learning of history that people can reflect. The Qur'an states: "So relate to them stories perhaps they may reflect." (Qur'an 7:176)[96] Also: "We are relating to you the most beautiful of the stories in that we have revealed to you from the Qur'an, though before it you were among those who were not aware of them." (Qur'an 12:3)[97] Again, the Qur'an states: "There is, indeed, in their stories lessons for people endowed with understanding. It is not any invented tale, but a confirmation of what went before it, and a detailed exposition of all things and a guide and a mercy to the people who believe."(Qur'an 12:111)[98] Based on these verses, storytelling has a high place in Islamic Culture within families. Children are told stories of the Prophets and other events that took place in the history preceding the revelation of the Qur'an.

INTERPRETATION OF DREAMS

Although the issue of dreams is a psychological issue, on the basis of cultural anthropology, it comes under the study of culture. Dreaming in Islamic culture is not a superstitious matter, but rather a scientific principle, because it has been mentioned in the Qur'an. As a matter of fact, the interpretation of dream has been given to the Prophet Yusuf (Joseph) as a gift of God. Hence dreaming and interpretation of dream is a fact of human culture and it has paramount value in Islamic life. The Qur'an says relating to the story of Prophet Yusuf (Joseph), "The man from

---

[96] Qur'an 7:176
[97] Qur'an 12:3
[98] Qur'an 12:111

Egypt who bought him said to his wife: Tend graciously to his dwelling. He may benefit us, or we may take him as a son. And thus did We establish Joseph in the land, that We might teach him of the interpretations of events that dreams foretell. For God prevails in His affairs. But most people do not comprehend this." (Qur'an 12:21)[99] God Almighty gave the news of entering to Masjid Al Haram to the Prophet in his dream. Allah says in the Qur'an, "Very truly, with profound truth God has confirmed His Messenger's true vision, as seen in his dream, of entering the Sacred Mosque in security: You shall certainly enter the Sacred Mosque, by the will of God, in full security, with your heads ceremonially shaved or hair shortened, without any fear. For He knows what you do not know. Moreover, He has decreed, apart from this, another imminent victory for you." (Qur'an 48:27)[100] The story of Prophet Abraham in the Qur'an is also evidence of dream and its interpretation in Islamic culture. The Qur'an says, "So when he had attained to an age of striving with him in good works, Abraham said: O my dear son! I have seen in a dream that I am to sacrifice you. So consider this, and tell me what you think? He said: O my dear father! Do what you are commanded by God. You shall find me, if God so wills, among those who are patient." (Qur'an 37:102)[101] The above verses clearly indicates the spiritual, metaphysical and intellectual position of dreams in the Islamic culture and that is why Muslims take dreams very seriously. It has been recommended that Muslims should go to bed with ablution and prayers so they should dream *al roya al saliha* (righteous dream). Abdullah Ibn Abbas reported from the Prophet of Islam who said that a righteous dream is a revelation from God to a believing servant of Allah who informs him of the good and bad that will reach him soon and Allah will make him

---

[99] Qur'an 12:21
[100] Qur'an 48:27
[101] Qur'an 37:102

aware so he should not be selfish and not be fooled and be negligent of God's command. According to Muslim scholars, dream and dreaming is a natural process of the mind and brain. They indicated that dreams are of two kinds: one, that will tell about the truth of the affairs and second, that reveals the end of the affairs. They are in four categories. First, a commanding dream, is when somebody has been commanded to perform something as in the case of Abraham. Second, a withholding dream inspires to not perform something. Third, a forewarning dreams warns people of some incident or event. In this case, people should give charity, repent and make supplication. Fourth, a mubashir means spreader of good news. This is in the case of Mariam the mother of Jesus. If people dream of bad things it has been recommended that they should recite verse 255 of chapter 2 which is considered to be one of the most powerful verse in the Qur'an and many Muslims have memorized this at an early age, it follows: "God! There is no God but Him, the All-living, the Self-subsisting All- sustaining One. Slumber does not overtake Him, nor does sleep. To Him belongs all that is in the heavens and all that is in the Earth. Who is that shall intercede with Him, except by His permission? He knows what lies before them and what lies behind them. And they do not comprehend anything of His knowledge- except that which He wills." (Qur'an 2:255)[102] Interpretation of dreams in Islam is not the work of psychic or fortune tellers but purely men of knowledge who attain not only Qur'anic knowledge but also are very much pure in his heart and his actions are aligned with the tradition of the Prophet and he is aloof from worldly gains and a materialistic life.

---

[102] Qur'an 2:255

TRAVELING

Traveling is an important, eye-opening and vital principle of Islam culturally. The Prophet migrated from Mecca to Medina and established a sociopolitical order based on knowledge, obedience of God and Justice. The Islamic calendar starts with Hijra (migration). Muslims travelled to spread faith through caravan of commerce and doing business. As a matter of fact, Islam spread not by sword but by travelling and doing business with other people around the world. God commands people when they are oppressed and their rights are violated. The land of God is vast and they should leave and settle somewhere else as the Qur'an says, "Entire ways of life have already passed away in the generations before you, O humanity. So journey in the Earth, and see how devastating was the end of those who belied God!" (Qur'an 3:137)[103] One reason, from a cultural and anthropological point of view, that Hajj is one of the five pillars of Islam is because traveling makes people encounter, establish relationship, and make peoples mind open for more discovery and exploration. As we said earlier, it is through traveling that people start appreciating what they have and learn from others what is missing in their life. In short, according to Islam, traveling makes a person grow intellectually, economically, spiritually, and socially.

---

[103] Qur'an 3:137

PART EIGHT

MYSTICISM

Mysticism

Mysticism in Islam is the highest level of wisdom in which one finds the true light of reality and love. As a matter of fact, it's a spiritual journey to reach God. No one can reach God, according to Islamic mysticism without the knowledge of the Qur'an or the tradition of the Prophet. It is not only pondering or thinking about the reality. It is through the understanding of the Qur'an and following the footsteps of the Prophet step by step that one may reach the level of wisdom. However, this cannot be done with only practices without clearing the mind and the heart for the sake of God. A Sufi is the one who lives for the sake of God alone. He is not after a worldly life and what he does is all for the sake of love of his Creator. It is through pure love that one can attain felicity. Annemarie Schimmel in her famous work on Mystical Dimensions of Islam writes, "Mysticism can be defined as love of the Absolute- for the power that separates true mysticism from mere asceticism is love. Divine love makes the seeker capable of bearing, even of enjoying, all the pains and afflictions that God showers upon him in order to test him and to purify his soul." (Page 4)[104]

SUFISM

In Sufism not only does the mystic find the Only Reality but also he finds himself in this universal system through a *tariqa* (which is the path). The path comes out of *sharia*. The one who walks through the path is a *salik* (that means wayfarer). The wayfarer, through his wondering reaches different stages to attain the

---

[104] Schimmel, Annemarie. *Mystical dimensions of Islam*

understanding of the total Tawhid. It is through sharia and tariqa that one reaches the consciousness of *marifa* (which means gnosis).

The following are the most prominent Muslim scholars who discuss Sufism in their lifetime, including Abdullah Ibn Mohammed ibn Abdul Wahhab.

Imam Abu Hanifa (81-150 H./700-767 CE)

Imam Abu Hanifa (85 H.-150 H) said, "If it were not for two years, I would have perished. For two years I accompanied Sayyidina Jafar as-Sadiq and I acquired the spiritual knowledge that made me a knower in the Way."

The book *Ad-Durr al-Mukhtar*, vol 1. p. 43, mentions that Ibn Abidin said, "Abi Ali Dakkak, one of the sufi saints, received his path from Abul Qassim an-Nasarabadi, who received it from ash-Shibli, who received it from Sariyy as-Saqati who received it from Maruf al-Karkhi, who received it from Dawud at-Ta'i, who received the knowledge, both the external and the internal, from the Imam Abu Hanifa, who was supporting the Sufi Spiritual Path." The Imam said before he died: *lawla sanatan lahalaka Numan*, "Were it not for a certain two years, Numan [i.e. myself] would have perished." There were the last two years of his life, when he began accompanying Jafar as-Sadiq.

Imam Malik (94-179 H./716-795 CE)

Muslim scholars unanimously approved of the mysticism in Islamic life. Imam Malik 716-795 C.E said, "Whoever studies jurisprudence (*fiqh*) and didn't study Sufism (*tasawwuf*) will be corrupted; and whoever studied tasawwuf and didn't study jurisprudence will become a heretic; and whoever combined both will be reach the Truth." This saying is mentioned and explained in the book of the scholar 'Ali al-Adawi with the explanation of Imam Abil-Hassan, a scholar of jurisprudence, vol. 2, p. 195.

Imam Shafi'i (150-205 H./767-820 CE)

Imam Shafi'i said, "I accompanied the Sufi people and I received from them three knowledges:

1. They taught me how to speak.
2. They taught me how to treat people with leniency and a soft heart.
3. They guided me in the ways of Sufism."

This is mentioned in the books, *Kashf al-Khafa* and *Muzid al-Albas,* by Imam 'Ajluni, vol. 1, p. 341.

Imam Ahmad bin Hanbal (164-241 H./780-855 CE)

Imam Ahmad (r) said, advising his son, "O my son, you have to sit with the People of Sufism, because they are like a fountain of knowledge and they keep the Remembrance of Allah in their hearts. They are the ascetics and they have the most spiritual power." This is explained in the book *Tanwir al-Qulub*, p. 405, by Shaikh Amin al-Kurdi.

Imam Ahmad said about the Sufis, as mentioned in the book *Ghiza al-Albab*, vol. 1, p. 120, "I don't know any people better than them."

Imam al-Muhasibi (d. 243 H./857 CE)

Imam al-Muhasibi reported that the Prophet (s) said, "My Nation is going to split into 73 divisions and only one of them will be the Group of Salvation." And Allah knows best that the Group is the people of *Tasawwuf.* He went deeply into the explanation of that subject, in the book *Kitab al-Wasiya* p. 27-32.

Imam al-Qushayri (d. 465 H./1072 CE)

Imam al-Qushayri said about Sufism, "Allah made this group the best of His saints and He honored them above all of His Servants after His Messengers and Prophets, and He made their hearts the secrets of His Divine Presence and He chose them from among the Nation to receive His Lights. They are the means of humanity. He cleaned them from all connections to this world, and He lifted them to the highest states of vision. And He unveiled to them the Realities of His Unique Oneness. He made them to observe His Will operating in them. He made them to shine in His Existence and to appear as Lights of His Lights." [*ar-Risalat al-Qushayriyya*, p. 2]

Imam Ghazali (450-505 H./1058-1111 CE)

Imam Ghazali, *Hujjat ul-Islam*, the Proof of Islam, said about Sufism, "I knew to be true that the Sufis are the seekers in Allah's Way, and that their conduct is the best conduct, and their way is the best way, and their manners are the most sanctified. They have cleaned their hearts from other than Allah and they have made them as pathways for rivers to run receiving knowledge of the Divine Presence." [*al-Munqidh min ad-Dalal*, p. 131]

Imam Nawawi (620-676 H./1223-1278 CE)

Imam Nawawi said, in his Letters, *al-Maqasid*, "The specifications of the way of the Sufis are five:

1. To keep the presence of Allah in your heart in public and in private;
2. To follow the Sunnah of the Prophet (s) by actions and speech;
3. To keep away from dependence on people;
4. To be happy with what Allah gives you, even if it is little;

5. To always refer your matters to Allah, Almighty and Exalted." [*Maqasid at-Tawhid*, p. 20]

Imam Fakhr ad-Din ar-Razi (544-606 H./1149-1209 CE)

Imam Fakhr ad-Din ar-Razi said, "The way the Sufis seek knowledge is to disconnect themselves from this worldly life, and keep themselves constantly busy in their mind and in their heart, with Dhikrullah, during all their actions and behaviors." [*Itiqadat Firaq al-Muslimin*, p. 72, 73]

Ibn Khaldun (733-808 H./1332-1406 CE)

Ibn Khaldun said, "The way of the Sufis is the way of the Salaf, the Scholars among the Sahahba, Tabiin, and Tabi at-Tabiin. Its origin is to worship Allah and to leave the ornaments of this world and its pleasures." [*Muqaddimat ibn Khaldun*, p. 328]

Tajuddin as-Subki

Tajuddin as-Subki (r) mentioned in his book *Muid an-Naim*, p. 190, under the chapter entitled *Sufism*, "May Allah praise them and greet them and may Allah make us to be with them in Paradise. Too many things have been said about them and too many ignorant people have said things which have no relation to them. And the truth is that they have left dunya and are busy with worship."

He said, "They are the People of Allah, whose dua and prayers Allah accepts, and by means of whom Allah supports human beings."

Jalaluddan as-Suyuti

He said in his book *Ta'yad al-Haqiqat al-Aliyya*, p. 57, "Sufism in itself is the best and most honorable knowledge. It explains how to follow the Sunnah of the Prophet (s) and to leave innovation."

Ibn Taymiyya (661-728 H./1263-1328 CE)

In *Majmaa Fatawa Ibn Taymiyya*, published by Dar ar-Rahmat, Cairo, Vol, 11, page 497, *Book of Tasawwuf*, Ibn Taymiyya says: "You have to know that the rightly-guided shaikhs must be taken as guides and examples in the Din, as they are following in the footsteps of the Prophets and Messengers. The Way (tariqat) of those shaikhs is to call people to Allah's Divine Presence and obedience to the Prophet."

Ibn Taymiyya says on page 499 of the same volume: "The shaikhs whom we need to take as guides are our examples and we have to follow them. As when on the Hajj (the pilgrimage), one needs a guide *(dalil)* to reach the Ka'aba, these shaikhs are our guide *(dalil)* to Allah and our Prophet (s)."

Among the shuyukh he mentioned are: Ibrahim ibn Adham, Maruf al-Karkhi, Hasan al-Basri, Rabia al-Adawiyya, Junaid ibn Mohammed, Shaikh Abdul Qadir Jilani, Shaikh Ahmad ar-Rafa'i, and Shaikh Bayazid al- Bistami.

Ibn Taymiyya quotes from Bayazid al-Bistami on page 510, Volume 10: "...the great Sufi shaikh, Bayazid al-Bistami, and the famous story of when he saw God in a vision *(kashf)* and said to Him: 'O Allah what is the way to You?' And Allah responded, 'Leave yourself and come to Me.'" Ibn Taymiyya continues quoting Bayazid al-Bistami, "I shed my self as a snake sheds its skin."

Implicit in this quotation is an indication of the need for *zuhd* (self-denial or abstention from the worldly life), as that was the path followed by Bayazid al-Bistami.

So we see from the above quotes, that Ibn Taymiyya was accepting many shaikhs by quoting them and urging people to follow guides to show the way to obey God and to obey the Prophet(s).

What Ibn Taymiyya Says About the Term *Tasawwuf*

"The crucible itself tells you, when you are strained, Whether you are gold or gold-plated copper." Sanai.

Following is what Ibn Taymiyya said about the definition of *Tasawwuf*, from Volume 11, *At-Tasawwuf*, of *Majmua Fatawa Ibn Taymiyya al-Kubra*, Dar ar-Rahmah, Cairo:

"Alhamdulillah, the use of the word tasawwuf has been thoroughly discussed. This is a term that was given to those who were dealing with that branch of knowledge *(tazkiyat an-nafs and Ihsan)*."

"*Tasawwuf* is the science of realities and states of experience. The Sufi is that one who purifies himself from everything which distracts him from the remembrance of Allah and who is so filled with knowledge of the heart and knowledge of the mind that the value of gold and stones will be equal to him. *Tasawwuf* safeguards the precious meanings and leaves behind the call to fame and vanity to reach the state of Truthfulness. The best of humans after the Prophets are the Siddiqin, as Allah mentioned them in Surat An-Nisa', 69: "All who obey Allah and the Messenger are in the company of those on whom is the grace of Allah: the Prophets, the sincere lovers of truth *(siddiqin)*, the martyrs and the righteous; Ah! what a beautiful fellowship.""

He continues about the Sufis, "They are striving to be obedient to Allah... So from them you will find the foremost in nearness by virtue of their striving. And some of them are from the people of the right hand..."

The Sufi Cloak (*khirqa*)

Before proceeding to Imam Ibn Qayyim, it may be useful to say something about the wearing of the Sufi cloak. In the view of the Trustworthy, there are three categories of shaikh:

1. The Shaikh of the Cloak
2. The Shaikh of the Dhikr
3. The Shaikh of Guidance

The first two categories (The Shaikh of the Cloak and The Shaikh of the Dhikr) are really deputies of a shaikh, representing the reality of the shaikh or the tariqat through the intermediary of either the cloak or the dhikr. The Shaikh of the Cloak (*Khirqah*) depends on the power of the cloak to act on the murid. The murid takes his support from the cloak, which a fully realized Shaikh of Guidance has imbued with his blessings.

The murid of the Shaikh of Dhikr is supported by the dhikr, not directly by the shaikh. In these two cases, the shaikh becomes the symbol, because the real support of the murid is the cloak or the dhikr.

The highest of the three categories is the Shaikh of Guidance. He is the one who supports the murid without any intermediary, directly from himself to the murid. He is the real shaikh because, without any means, he supports and directs the murid directly through his heart. That is why Sayyidina Ahmad al-Faruqi said, "In our tariqat the shaikh guides the murid directly, unlike other tariqats which use the cloak and other means to lift up their murids."

In the Naqshbandi Tariqat only one shaikh, the Shaikh of Guidance, is therefore accepted as possessing real authority. When that shaikh passes away, the murids must renew their initiation with his successor, to whom he has transmitted all his secrets and his inheritance from the Prophet(s) and all his predecessors in the Golden Chain.

Imam Ibn Qayyim (d. 751 H./1350 CE)

Imam Ibn Qayyim stated that, "We can witness the greatness of the people of *tasawwuf* in the eyes of the Salaf by what has been mentioned by Sufyan ath-Thawri (d. 161 H./777 CE). One of the greatest imams in the 2nd century and one of the foremost mujtahids, he said: "If not for Abu Hisham as-Sufi (d. 115 H./733 CE) I would never have perceived the action of the subtlest forms of hypocrisy *(riya')* in the self." *(Manazil as-Sa'ireen)*

Ibn Qayyim continues: "Among the best of people is the Sufi learned in fiqh."

Abdullah ibn Mohammed ibn Abdul Wahhab (1115-1201 H./1703-1787 CE)

Following is a quotation from Mohammed Man ar Numani's book (p. 85), *Ad-Dia'at al-Mukaththafa Didd ash-Shaikh Mohammed ibn Abdul Wahhab*: "Shaikh Abdullah, the son of shaikh Mohammed ibn Abdul Wahhab, said about *Tasawwuf*: "My father and I don't deny or criticize the Science of Sufism, but on the contrary we support it because it cleans the external and the internal of the hidden sins which are related to the heart and the outward form. Even though the individual might externally be on the right way, internally he might be on the wrong way; and for its correction *tasawwuf* is necessary."

In the fifth volume of the collection of letters by Mohammed ibn Abdul Wahhab entitled *ar-Rasa'il ash-Shakhsiyya,* page 11, and again on pages 12, 61, and 64, he states: "I never accused of unbelief Ibn Arabi or Ibn al-Farid for their Sufi interpretations."

Ibn Abidin

The great scholar, Ibn Abidin in his book *Rasa'il Ibn Abidin* (p. 172-173) states: "The seekers in this way don't hear except from the Divine Presence and they don't love any but Him. If they remember Him they cry. If they thank Him they are happy. If they find Him they are awake. If they see Him they will be relaxed. If they walk in His Divine Presence, they melt. They are drunk with His Blessings. May Allah bless them."

Shaikh Mohammed Abduh (1265-1323 H./1849-1905 CE)

He stated, "*Tasawwuf* appeared in the first century of Islam and it received a tremendous honor. It cleansed the self and straightened the conduct and gave knowledge to people from the wisdom and secrets of the Divine Presence." [quoted from *Majallat al-Muslim*, 6th ed., 1378 H, p. 24]

Shaikh Rashad Rida

He said, "Sufism was a unique pillar from the pillars of the religion. Its purpose was to cleanse the self and to take account of one's daily behavior and to raise the people to a high station of spirituality." [*Majallat al-Manar*, 1st year, p. 726]

Maulana Abul Hasan Ali an-Nadwi

Maulana Abul Hasan Ali an-Nadwi is a member of the Islamic-Arabic Society of India and Muslim countries. He said in his book, *Muslims in India*, written some years ago, p. 140-146, "These Sufis initiate people in Oneness and sincerity in following the Sunnah of the Prophet (s) and in repentance from their sins and in avoidance of every disobedience to Allah, Almighty and Exalted. Their guides encourage them to move in the way of perfect love of Allah."

"In Calcutta, India, everyday more than 1000 people are taking initiation into Sufism."

"Thanks to the influence of Sufi people, thousands and hundreds of thousands in India found their Lord and reached a state of perfection through the Islamic religion."

Abul Ala Mawdudi

He said in his book *Mabadi' al-Islam* (p. 17), "Sufism is a reality whose signs are the love of Allah and the love of the Prophet (s), where one absents oneself for their sake, and one is annihilated from anything other than them. It instructs how to follow in the footsteps of the Prophet(s)."

"*Tasawwuf* searched for sincerity of heart, purity of intention, and trustworthiness of obedience in all of an individual's actions."

"Shariah and Sufism: what is the similitude of the two? They are like the body and the soul. The body is the external shari'ah knowledge and the spirit is the internal knowledge."

In sum, Sufism, in the present as in the past, is the effective means for spreading the reality of Islam, extending the knowledge and understanding of spirituality, and fostering happiness and peace. With it man can find himself and, in so doing, find his Lord. With it man can improve, transform, and elevate himself, and find salvation from the ignorance of this world and its misguided pursuit of some materialistic fantasy. And Allah knows best what he intends for his servants.

Wali- Auliya (Friends of Allah)

Wali means who is a close friend of Allah and who is protected by Allah. Wali is the singular and Auliya is the plural of Wali. The Qur'an says, "Verily, the friends of God, no fear is upon them nor are they sad." (Qur'an 10:63)[105] A true Wali is submitted entirely to the will of Allah and his manners and behavior exemplify the Prophet of Islam. They reach a level of wisdom where they become guides for spiritual attainment. Auliya in Islam do not have any self-interest. Their service is for the sake of Allah only. It is for this reason that their existence and role playing in the Muslim community has been vital for centuries. Their guidance of people made Islam alive by the principles of Islam and the Qur'an and the true path has always been revitalized by their actions. Because of their sacrifice for the sake of Allah and the people, they have a special place and position in the site of Allah. It is because of their high *maqa'm* (status) that they are allowed by God, as He wills, to intercede for people.

Proofs of Intercession and Meditation in the Qur'an and Hadith

Linguistic definitions Shafa`a is the Arabic noun for intercession or mediation or asking forgiveness from Allah for someone else. The word is used also in laying a petition before a king, interceding for a debtor, and in judicial procedure: "Whoso makes a righteous intercession shall partake of the good that ensues therefrom, and whoso makes an evil intercession will bear the consequence thereof;" (Qur'an 4:85)[106] "He who by his intercession invalidates one of Allah's *hudud* (laws concerning transgressions) is challenging (*tahadda*) Allah." (Bukhari, Anbiya' ch. 54) He who makes intercession is called *shafi`* and *shaf*.

---

[105] Qur'an 10:63
[106] Qur'an 4:85

Statement of the Doctrine of Intercession in Islam and the Obligations of Belief Therein Hujjat al-Islam Imam Ghazali said:

"It is obligatory to believe in the intercession of first, the Prophets, then religious scholars, then martyrs, then other believers, the intercession of each one commensurate with his rank and position with Allah Most High."

"Allah Himself is witness that there is no God save Him. And the angels and the men of learning too are witness" (Qur'an 3:18)[107] and "Whoso obey Allah and the Messenger, they are with those unto whom Allas has shown favor, of the Prophets and the saints and the martyrs and the righteous. The best of company are they!" (Qur'an 4:69)[108] Any believer remaining in hell without an intercessor shall be taken out of it by the favor of Allah, no one who believes remaining in it forever, and anyone with an atom's weight of faith in his heart will eventually depart from it.

PROOFS OF INTERCESSION AND MEDITATION IN THE QUR'AN

In the Holy Qur'an intercession is:

- a. negated in relation to the unbelievers,
- b. established categorically as belonging to Allah,
- c. further defined as generally permitted for others than Allah by His permission,
- d. further specified as permitted for the angels on behalf of whomever Allah wills,

---

[107] Qur'an 3:18
[108] Qur'an 4:69

e. explicitly attributed to the Prophet in his lifetime,
f. alluded to in reference to the Prophet in the afterlife, and
g. alluded to in reference to the generality of the Prophets and the believers in the afterlife.

To elaborate more, we quote directly from the Qur'an about the issue of intercession. Bear in mind, there are many people in Islamic Culture that see intercession of Auliya as valid and there are people based on the following verses, who see it as invalid. What is important anthropologically is that both groups exist and believe in Allah and the Day of Judgment.

The Day of Judgment is described as a day on which no intercession will be accepted from the Children of Israel (2:48) or the unbelievers generally speaking (2:254), or the idolaters (10:18,74:48):

- 2:48: "And guard yourselves against a day when no soul will avail another, nor intercession be accepted from it."

- 2:254: "O believers, spend of that wherewith We have provided you before a day come when there will be no trafficking, nor friendship, nor intercession. The disbelievers, they are the wrong-doers."

- 10:19: "They worship beside Allah that which neither hurteth them nor profiteth them, and they say: These are our intercessors with Allah."

- 74:48: "The mediation of no mediators will avail them then."

In absolute terms intercession belongs to Allah alone:

- 39:43-44: "Or choose they intercessors other than Allah? Say: What! Even though they have power over nothing and have no intelligence? Say: the intercession belongs to Allah."

A further definition that "Intercession belongs to Allah" is that intercession is actually permitted to some others than Allah but only by His permission:

- 2:255: "Who should intercede with him, except by his permission?"

- 10:4: "There is no intercessor save after His permission."

- 19:87: "They will have no power of intercession, save him who has made a covenant with his Lord."

- 43:86: "And those unto whom they cry instead of Him possess no power of intercession, except him who beareth witness unto the truth knowingly."

Angels are permitted to intercede for whomever Allah wills, specifically among the believers:

- 21:26-28: "And they say: the Beneficent hath taken unto Himself a son... Nay, but honored slaves [angels]... and they cannot intercede except for him whom He accepted, and they quake for awe of Him."

- 40:7: "Those who bear the Throne, and all who are round about it... ask forgiveness for those who believe."

- 42:5: "The angels hymn the praise of their Lord and ask forgiveness for those on the Earth."

The intercession of the Prophet in his lifetime is explicitly and frequently established:

- 3:159: "Pardon them and ask forgiveness for them and consult with them upon the conduct of affairs."

- 4:64: "And if, when they had wronged themselves, they had but come unto thee and asked forgiveness of Allah, and the Messenger had asked forgiveness for them, they would have found Allah forgiving, merciful."

- 4:106-107: "And ask forgiveness of Allah (for others). Allah is ever forgiving, merciful. And plead not on behalf of those who deceive themselves."

- 8:33: "But Allah would not punish them while thou wast with them, nor will He punish them while they seek forgiveness."

- 9:80, 84: "Ask forgiveness for them (the hypocrites) or ask not forgiveness for them; though thou ask forgiveness for them seventy times Allah will not forgive them... And never pray for one of them who dieth, nor stand by his grave."

- 9:103: "Pray for them. Lo! Thy prayer is an assuagement for them."

- 9:113: "It is not for the Prophet, and those who believe, to pray for the forgiveness of idolaters even though they may be near of kin (to them) after it hath become clear that they are people of hell-fire."

- 24:62: "If they ask thy leave for some affair of theirs, give leave to whom thou wilt of them, and ask for them forgiveness of Allah."

- 47:19: "Know that there is no god save Allah, and ask forgiveness for thy sin and for believing men and believing women."

- 60:12: "Accept their [believing women's] allegiance and ask Allah to forgive them."

- 63:5-6: "And when it is said unto them: Come! the messenger of Allah will ask forgiveness for you, they [the hypocrites] avert their faces and thou seest them turning away, disdainful. Whether thou ask forgiveness for them or ask not forgiveness for them, Allah will not forgive them."

The intercession and mediation of the Prophet on the Day of Judgment has been established by the consensus of scholars (ijma`), where belief in the Day of Judgment is an article of belief in Islam as stated in Section (2). The Mu`tazili reject it, as they hold that the man who enters the Fire will remain there forever. The consensus of scholars is based on the principle of permission (see the verses in Section (3.c) above), on the allusive

verses in the present section, and on the more explicit Hadiths quoted further below:

- 17:79: "It may be that thy Lord will raise thee to a Praised Station."

- 93:5: "And verily thy Lord will give unto thee so that thou wilt be content."

The intercession of the generality of the Prophets as well as the believers has similarly been established by the verses of Sections (3.c) and (3.e) above, i.e., based on permission, and also because Prophets have made a covenant with their Lord (33:7, 3:81) and do bear witness unto the truth knowingly. The latter is true also of the elite of the believers (3:18: "Allah, the angels, and the men of learning"). There are also the following verses concerning the Prophets' intercession in their lifetime:

- 12:97-98: "And they said: O our father! Ask forgiveness of our sins for us for lo! we were sinful. And he [Jacob] said: I shall ask forgiveness for you of my Lord. He is the forgiving, the merciful."

- 19:47: "He [Abraham] said: Peace unto thee. I shall ask forgiveness of my Lord for thee."

- 61:4: "Abraham promised his father: I will ask forgiveness for thee, though I owe nothing for thee from Allah."

There are also the following verses concerning the believers' intercession in their lifetime:

- 9:113: "It is not for the Prophet, and those who believe, to pray for the forgiveness of idolaters even though they may be near of kin (to them) after it hath become clear that they are people of hellfire."
- 59:10: "And those who came after them say: Our Lord! forgive us and forgive our believing brothers who lived before us."

PROOFS OF INTERCESSION AND MEDITATION IN THE HADITH

In the Hadith, the power of intercession is emphasized as given:

    a. to the Prophet exclusively of other Prophets;
    b. to special members of the Prophet's community, such as saints and scholars;
    c. to the common believers of the Prophet's community.

Intercession of the Prophet:

    In his lifetime for those who passed away:

        All the authentic traditions concerning the Prophet's prayer and takbir over the graves of the believers."

        Muslim [jana'iz]: Abu Hurayra narrates that a dark-complexioned woman or young man used to sweep the mosque. When that person died, no-one told the Prophet until he enquired about it and then went to pray over the grave. He remarked: "Verily, these graves are full of darkness for their dwellers. Verily, Allah Mighty and Glorious illumines them for their occupants by reason of my prayer for them."

Muslim: "Whoever repeats after the words of the mu'adhdhin, my intercession will be guaranteed for him."

Tirmidhi (hasan gharib) and Ibn Hibban: "Those closest to me in the Hereafter are those who invoked blessings upon me the most (in dunya)."

Bukhari and Muslim: Jabir narrated that the Prophet said: "I have been given five things which no Prophet was given before me: I was made victor over my enemies through fear struck in their heart; I was permitted to take the booty of war; The whole Earth was made a place of prostration for me and its soil ritually pure, so when the time to pray comes upon anyone of my community, let him pray there and then; I was given shafa`a (intercession/mediation with Allah); Every Prophet was sent to his people in particular and I was sent to all peoples."

Ahmad and Tabarani (hasan): Burayda narrates that the Prophet said: "Verily I shall intercede on the Day of Judgment for more men than there are stones and clods of mud on the Earth."

Bukhari and Muslim: Abu Hurayra narrates a long Hadith wherein the Prophet intercedes and his intercession is accepted when all other

Prophets are powerless to intercede. In al-Hasan's version in Bukhari, the Prophet intercedes and is accepted for four types of people: For those who have a grain of faith in their heart;
For those who have a mustard seed of faith in their heart;
For those who have less than that of faith in their heart;
For those who ever said: la ilaha illAllah.

PART NINE

DEATH AND FUNERAL

DEATH

Human life, according to Islam ends with death but this death is not his/her eternal death. As a matter of fact, according to the Qur'an, a person will be raised again after death and start his eternal life. Death in Islam is not a disaster but is a blessing of Allah because naturally one leaves this life and joins Him. The Qur'an says, "Those who when an affliction strikes them, say: Indeed, to God do we belong, and indeed to Him are we returning." (Qur'an 2:156)[109] Also those who are killed in the path of God are called martyrs, such as Imam Hussein, and they are always alive in the memory of the living. The Qur'an says, "Thus you shall not say, regarding those whore are killed in the path of God, that they are dead. Rather, they are alive! But you cannot perceive it." (Qur'an 2:154)[110] Also, it is important to note that in Islam, death does not come before the time is up. In other words, every individual has a specific time in this life and when the time is due, then for a variety of pretexts, he leaves this world at a specific time. This is called ajal. There is no death without ajal, and the Qur'an says the date and time is fixed as such: "Nor can a soul die except by Allah's leave; the term being fixed as by Decree." (Qur'an 3:145)[111]

According to Islam, what one takes with him/her from this life is his/her deed and creed, and nothing else. Believing in this principle that people leave this world with a white piece of shroud but nothing else makes the funeral very simple and inexpensive. It is prohibited to use expensive caskets or dress

---

[109] Qur'an 2:156
[110] Qur'an 2:154
[111] Qur'an 3:145

people with expensive suits and make them wear jewelry. Muslims are buried with three pieces of white cloth as a shroud.

FUNERAL PROCEDURE

Funeral prayer is not like regular prayer. The Imam stands in front of the casket in the middle and facing the Ka'aba' and recites four takbirs. There is no call for prayer, there is no bowing or prostration. The prayer can take place inside or outside the mosque.

The body is washed (wudhu and ghusul) three or five times and then perfume is used on the body called Sidr. Next, they sprinkle some camphor before shrouding. Shrouding comes last in two or three pieces. The casket should be made of a very inexpensive wood and should be nail-less. Camphor is used as an antiseptic and a nail-less casket is used because of environmental issues so as not to pollute the land. Actually, according to the tradition of the Prophet, there is no casket required and the body should be laid down, wrapped up with the shroud made of pure cotton in the ground on Earth. This way, when the body is decomposed, it will not pollute the land. Nowadays, environmentalists search different way to come up with coffins that dissolve in the Earth while in Islam this was practiced fourteen hundred years ago. In most cases currently, non-Muslims are buried in coffins. The interior of these coffins contain formaldehyde, hydrochloric acids, dioxins, and other toxic chemicals. In essence, they are burying their loved ones in a toxic environment that is also seriously polluting the Earth. Environmentalists, today, have created eco-friendly or green coffins that are environmentally safe and biodegradable. This is a case of environmental anthropology that is highly important in our studies.

The casket is carried by people over their shoulders to the graveyard. When putting the casket in the grave, the body is placed resting on its right side or on their back with the face towards Ka'aba. After the burying is complete, there is a short sermon by a person who is well versed in Islamic knowledge with recitation of the Qur'an and supplication for the dead person so that Allah may forgive him in the Hereafter and grant him paradise. It is important to note that both men and women can join funeral prayer and women can also accompany in the funeral procession as long as they are properly dressed and control their emotions. The main reason women are occasionally forbidden to accompany the funeral procession to the grave is because women sometimes wail aloud and show emotions that actually disturb the soul of the dead person. Hadith number 368 of Sahih Bukhari narrated that Om Atiyya has said, "We were forbidden to accompany funeral procession but not strictly."(Book of Funeral- Al Bukhari)[112] The Prophet of Islam prohibited the wailing, screaming, slapping of one's face, and tearing clothes in a funeral by women. As a matter of fact, the Prophet said, "He who slaps the cheeks, tears his/her clothes, and follows the tradition of the days of ignorance is not from us."

---

[112] Hadith 368, Sahih Al Bukhari

Conclusion

According to Muslims, believing in the Qur'an and the traditions of the Prophet of Islam, makes Islam a complete way of life. In this study, we brought the cultural aspects of the Islamic way of living and, in particular, the cultural anthropology of Islam. Islamic Culture, which has been designed by revelation in the Qur'an and by the Prophet's sayings and practices, not only gives a cultural identity to a person, but also, enriches him or her with norms and values that complete a human being from birth to death, which is the study of ontology. Hopefully, in another book, we will cover this more in depth in the future. There is a mystery about Islamic Culture that, despite all other cultural invasions throughout history, Muslims, by believing in their Creator and the leadership of the Prophet, preserved their culture. The Soviet Union, in their seventy years of Communist rule, tried to deculturize Muslims in Russia but they failed. Ataturk, the father of modern-day Turkey, brought secularism to Turkey and he tried to wipe out the cultural identity of Turkish Muslims, but, as we can see today, he failed. After two hundred years of colonialism in the Middle East, Muslims are paying high sacrifices for their cultural identity under the name of democracy and freedom. The simple formula for the richness of this culture throughout history is simply believing in one God, and that, according to the Qur'an, "We came from Him and we return to Him."

References

1. Cleary, Thomas. *The Essential Koran*. San Francisco: Harper, 1993.

2. Boisard, Marcel A. *Humanism in Islam*, Page 34. American Trust Publication, 1988. Print.

3. "How Were Hadith Compiled." *CPS Global* N.p., n.d. Web. 1 February 2013. <http://www.cpsglobal.org/content/how-were-Hadith-compiled>

4. Ismail, Muttaqi. "Articles of Faith in Islam." *Islamic Learning Materials* N.p., 28 December 2009. Web. 3 March 2013. <http://islamiclearningmaterials.com/articles-of-faith-in-Islam/>

5. "Daily Duas." *Read With Tajweed* N.p., n.d. Web. 12 December 2012. <http://www.readwithtajweed.com/daily_duas.htm>

6. "Search Truth." *Search Truth* N.p., n.d. Web. 8 August 2012. <http://www.searchtruth.com/searchHadith.php?keyword=Istikhara&translator=1&search=1&book=&start=0&records_display=20&search_word=all>

7. Ebrahim, Abul Fadl M. *Abortion, Birth Control, and Surrogate Parenting: An Islamic Perspective*. American Trust Publication, 1989. Print.

8. Schimmel, Annemarie. *Mystical dimensions of Islam*. The University of North Carolina Press, 1975. Print.